Joyful **Noise**

ALSO BY RICK MOODY

Purple America
The Ring of Brightest Angels
  Around Heaven
The Ice Storm
Garden State

ALSO BY DARCEY STEINKE

Jesus Saves
Suicide Blonde
Up Through the Water

Joyful Noise

The New Testament Revisited

Edited by Rick Moody and Darcey Steinke

Little, Brown and Company

Boston   New York   Toronto   London

FIRST EDITION

Library of Congress Cataloging-in-Publication Data

Joyful noise : the New Testament revisited / edited by Rick Moody and
    Darcey Steinke. — 1st ed.
            p.   cm.
    Includes bibliographical references.
    ISBN 0-316-57928-9
    1. Bible. N.T. — Criticism, interpretation, etc. I. Moody, Rick.
II. Steinke, Darcey.
BS2395.J69   1997
225.6 — DC21   97-19497

10   9   8   7   6   5   4   3   2   1

MV-NY

Published simultaneously in Canada by Little, Brown & Company
(Canada) Limited

PRINTED IN THE UNITED STATES OF AMERICA

Contents

Contents

Joyful **Noise**

*For the Reverend John W. Moody and
the Reverend Paul David Steinke,
with special thanks to all at the
Long Island Restaurant*

Introduction
The Parable of the
Hidden Treasure

Rick Moody

EVERY generation interprets the Bible for itself.

In some quarters, even this initial proposition is perilous. But if it's so with works of literature, why not the Bible? If *Moby-Dick* is wordy nonsense in one generation ("The first thing which must be said of Melville," wrote Leonard Woolf in 1923, "is that he writes the most execrable English") and a great work of art the next, isn't it possible to find the same shifting of responses in the case of the Bible? Of course, there's already a tremendous range of beliefs among biblical interpreters at any single moment. For example, what to make of the conflicting interpretations of the Book of Revelation in the Middle Ages and after? What to make of the writings known as the Apocrypha, canonized by Catholics but not by some Protestant branches of the Christian Church? And if there's this range of interpretations in an age, why not between the generations?

This book attempts a slightly rash demonstration: that within the generation presently arriving in the fullness of adulthood, as within Christian denominations, as within the culture at large, there are particular strains of thinking about belief that reveal our contemporary theological trends. Some of these trends may be manifest in sacred or inspired investigations, as in the sustained textual studies of the moment (the Jesus Seminar, for example, a group of scholars attempting to establish the "truth" of various quotations and works attributed to Jesus), or they may be manifest in secular interpretations, as in *Godspell* or *Jesus Christ Superstar* — two sources of lay interpretation that, as these essays will demonstrate, have nonetheless been important proselytizing forces for younger Americans. But, whether sacred or profane, popular or specialized, spirituality is still engaged by my contemporaries in ways that are vital and relevant.

The spectrum of current biblical interpretations makes sense when you think about the hodgepodge fashion in which the New Testament was composed in the first place. This is most evident, recently, in the scholarship on the so-called Sayings Gospel of Q. According to twentieth-century theologians, the Gospel writers called Matthew and Luke both relied upon a single compendium of sayings attributed to Jesus (e.g., Matthew 6:28, "Consider the lilies of the field, how they grow; they toil not, neither do they spin," which reappears identically in Luke). This compendium of sayings, called Q, when combined with Mark's biographical narrative of Christ, accounts mostly for the synoptic Gospels, for Matthew and Luke and Mark, as we recognize them these days. Yet this theory of Q implies that in spite of the seductive notion that the Gospels were written by eyewitnesses to Jesus' ministry and are thus immutable, it is more likely that there were, after Christ's death, a number of different gospels and testaments, per-

haps even competing texts.* Moreover, according to contemporary theologians, Q itself is constructed in different layers, with
different themes according to the different needs of first-century
spiritual communities. Of these layers of Q, I'm personally drawn
to the first and earliest, which depicts a forgiving and tolerant
Jesus of Nazareth, a Cynic-Philosopher Jesus. Of him, we have
the following: "Love your enemies, do good to them which hate
you" (Luke 6:27), and also, "And unto him that smiteth thee on
the one cheek offer also the other; and him that taketh away thy
cloak forbid not to take thy coat also" (Luke 6:29).

It follows that some of the writing about Jesus of Nazareth was
entirely independent of the synoptic Gospels. The Johannine Gospel (with its lovely, almost Gnostic proem, as discussed later in these
pages), the Sayings Gospel of Q, the Gnostic Gospel of Thomas,
and so on may have involved ideas of who Jesus was that differ
considerably from Christ as he is most often characterized in the
modern church. The implication here is self-evident. If the Bible
itself doesn't have a definitive shape, if the very construction of the
Bible itself is subject to debate, can we hold fast to the proposition
that its interpretations should be singular, orthodox, or fixed?

My belief is that the Bible has to be *open* — as the word is
used, for example, by Umberto Eco: "*Every* work of art, even
though it is produced by following an explicit or implicit poetics
of necessity, is effectively open to a virtually unlimited range of
possible readings, each of which causes the work to acquire new
vitality in terms of one particular taste, or perspective." What
perspective other than openness is there for contemporary readers

---

* I'm borrowing here from Burton L. Mack's *Who Wrote the New Testament: The
Making of the Christian Myth* and *The Lost Gospel: The Book of Q and Christian
Origins.*

with respect to a text that itself borrows its first five chapters from another book (the Pentateuch) and then claims to have fulfilled or in some cases even superseded this preliminary text? How else to regard a book loaded with spurious authorial attributions, with ambiguous poetry, with mixed ambitions, with (occasionally) inconsistently applied theology?

Though I've been a sort of armchair hermeneuticist for some years, the idea for this anthology came suddenly and organically, at a dinner party, in the midst of a conversation about the contemporary hegemony of the religious right. That night, I blurted out to friends the thought that the only way to oppose these conservative moralizers was to engage in a debate about the meaning of the New Testament. The idea stuck with me, and I continued to argue with others that it wasn't exclusively the Christian aspects of the New Testament that were important for contemporary Americans, as it was not *only* that Martin Luther King Jr. was an advocate of civil rights that made his program heroic, or only that Gandhi was the architect of Indian independence. It is the broad moral significance of King's and Gandhi's accomplishments — their leadership, their thoughtfulness, their consistency — that lives on. The same is true of Jesus of Nazareth. Jesus, in addition to any of his other accomplishments, was a great moral thinker.

My generation often abdicates its responsibilities when faced with the chance to articulate what it believes, whether these beliefs are Christian or of any other stripe. Certain cadres are willing to speak up — as with the admirable crusades, lately, for gay rights, equal rights for women, or rights for disabled persons. But regarding what might be ethically universal among contemporary humankind, my coevals have little to say. Universals are slippery and difficult for those of us educated in the liberal tradition. A healthy disrespect for the moral vision and leadership of institutionalized religion and pseudoreligious political opportunists is the norm. Yet ethical and spiritual values are nonetheless implied among my peers — by a dislike for suffering, a belief in equality and justice generally, a desire to redress past political or social errors, and so forth. Values are there. It's just that few are willing to discuss them, especially not in religious or spiritual terms.

The New Testament, of course, isn't reticent on universals. Think of the list of Beatitudes from Jesus' Sermon on the Mount. Or of Jesus' famous commentary on the commandments (Matthew 22:37–40 and Luke 10:27), "Thou shalt love the Lord thy God with all thy heart, and with all thy soul, and with all thy mind. This is the first and great commandment. And the second is like unto it, Thou shalt love thy neighbor as thyself. On these two commandments hang all the law and the prophets." As I began to think about these universals, and to think about the Gospels as great liberal documents in strong support of ethical universals, I was also beginning a dialogue with my coeditor, Darcey Steinke, in which we frequently discussed religious issues. Darcey and I each come from a background rich with religion and talk of faith, so these conversations derived their initial energy from a shared heritage. We covered a wide range of "spiritual" subjects: Lutheranism, Episcopalianism, Gnosticism, the existence of Evil (or lack thereof), the necessity for good works, etc. And in the course of time, our idea for an anthology of essays on the New Testament cohered.

It seemed to us that for many of our contemporaries, a wariness of the *spiritus mundi* originated in a perceived lack of options with respect to the moral debates of the day. Whatever the cause, this frequent inattention to religious heritage among young people has had a distinctly political effect. When liberals avoid a debate, they cede the terms of this debate to more conservative voices. Thus, the right and the far right in American culture have by now assumed almost entirely the mantle of interpreting the Bible and its implications for Americans. In our view, this Bible of the Right is long on the repressive, the intolerant, the punitive, the rigidly fundamentalist — especially as these aspects of morality are defined in the Old Testament, in the Book of Revelation, in some of the Pauline Epistles of the New Testament (e.g., 2 Corinthians 12:21: "I shall bewail many which have sinned already, and have not repented of the uncleanness and fornication and lasciviousness which they have committed," or Colossians 3:5: "Mortify therefore your members which are upon the earth: fornication, uncleanness, inordinate affection, evil concupiscence, and covetousness, which is idolatry; For which things' sake the wrath of God cometh on the children of disobedience"). To Darcey and me, and to many of our contemporaries — perhaps even among a silent majority — this punishing model doesn't square with our experience of spirituality, with the celebration, with the forgiveness, with the "good news" promised in the Gospels and in much of the rest of the New Testament.

The religion I inherited is joyful, personal, and full of the human passions, though these passions be disordered, occasionally homely, or sometimes even misguided. Yet this kind of forgiving moral scaffolding is attacked or mostly disregarded by fundamentalist Christianity in a sort of steroid-induced inflexibility about family, sexuality, and belief. The time is right, I think, to try to reorganize this debate, to enter into it thoughtfully, and to provide a voice and a platform for a different model of ethics — the absolving, human model — available to all men or women, whether or not they believe in a post-Easter Christ, or perhaps in religion at all.

Our format here, the anthology, is a way of collecting a range of evidence of a pragmatic New Testament morality, a religious morality somewhat in the shape described by William James in *The Varieties of Religious Experience,* or in the style of Thomas Jefferson's idiosyncratic and personal Bible. This anthology, therefore, is not a book written by biblical exegetes (though, as one of our contributors put it, the Bible wasn't written by biblical exegetes either): while we knew what we *didn't* want to include here — a repressive interpretation of Christianity — we were otherwise not interested in limiting points of view. We didn't shy away from ethics and religious history and interpretation, but we did not concentrate our attentions there exclusively. We have collected here essays by contemporary novelists, poets, scholars, artists — layfolk all — because this gives us the best opportunity to explore the range of voices and styles of this non-fundamentalist Christian spirituality. These voices include those of Jews and Buddhists and African Americans and Hispanic Americans and gay people, even a few mainline white Christians. We are mostly young.* This is an effort in the direction, therefore, of an unapologetically inclusive book. A book about how people really live now, in this difficult moment in the history of religion. A political book.

The preeminent suggestion we made to the contributors of this volume was not about doctrine — about belief in *incarnation* or about the orthodoxy of the Nicene Creed or even about the idea of Christ as Son of God. We suggested only that each writer deal, in some way, with the *text* of the New Testament, whether directly or intuitively. With its words. I'd like, finally, in inviting you into the essays that follow, to briefly step into this terrain

* There are a couple of over-fifty writers in this volume, but we're not going to single them out. Their essays amount to a kind of leadership in this contested landscape.

myself.* The following comes from the Gospel According to Matthew, chapter 13, the motherlode of poetical language and parabolic constructions by Jesus of Nazareth: "Again, the kingdom of heaven is like unto treasure hid in a field; the which when a man hath found, he hideth, and for joy thereof goeth and selleth all that he hath, and buyeth that field" (Matt. 13:44).

Interpretation of the New Testament parables has classically taken one of two directions. The first of these is strictly allegorical, in which every element of the parable can be translated, one-to-one, into facts of a second narrative. Usually in this allegorical reading the parable becomes a direct commentary on, or a prediction of, Christ's Passion. In fact, even Christ himself falls into this allegorical trap occasionally (probably when he's serving as the mouthpiece for later redactors), as in his instructions to the apostles on decoding the parable of the sower (Matt. 13:3–9): "The field is the world; the good seed are the children of the kingdom; but the tares are the children of the wicked one; the enemy that sowed them is the devil; the harvest is the end of the world; and the reapers are the angels" (Matt. 13:39).

An opposed but also important interpretive method among theologians is the so-called *rule of end stress* in parabolic construction,† in which the bulk of the parable is seen as realistic setting, existing only as backdrop for *the message,* which comes, conveniently, at the end of the parable, as in good storytelling.

---

* It was the novelist Jonathan Franzen who suggested to me the beauty and mystery of the parables, which I'm taking up here. My reading is informed by his model, and by an interpretation I first encountered in a sermon by the rector of Grace Church, Brooklyn, the Reverend Nils Blatz.

† See, e.g., *Interpreting the Parables,* by Archibald M. Hunter, Philadelphia: The Westminster Press, 1960.

My own interpretation of the parable of the hidden treasure is, somewhat ironically, rigidly allegorical (so that I might — like Mithridates — by using a dram of rigidity, steel myself against its poison): the treasure at the heart of this story *is the message of the kingdom itself,* and the fact of grace offered therein — grace in spite of the way you have lived your life, grace in spite of your crimes or your peccadilloes, grace in spite of your religion, grace in spite of mean birth or lofty one, grace in spite of your sexuality or the color of your skin or your creed or anything else, grace simply because grace is what God gives. That's the message buried in the New Testament, as treasure is buried in a field, the message often overpowered by the fire and brimstone of evangelists going all the way back to the destruction of the temple in Jerusalem, through two long millennia of Swaggarts and Robertsons. The Kingdom of Heaven, as opposed to the kingdom of PACs, multinationals, gun lobbyists, tax-exempt charitable corporations, et al., *is a place of grace,* and this is born out, moreover, by the fact that the protagonist of the parable of the hidden treasure is a reprobate. The treasure, after all, is in somebody else's field when he finds it. The treasure belongs to somebody else. So what kind of a guy is this, who has hidden the veritable kingdom of heaven so that he can come back later and swipe it?

He's like all of us.

And in my allegorical interpretation, this hit-and-run, morally dubious miscreant is myself, and the other writers and thinkers in this volume, and perhaps he is all of our contemporaries, those of us from a secular generation, from pockets of culture baldly "sinful" according to our orthodox brethren, who come here — to the realm of spiritual investigation — to claim the treasure for ourselves, to steal it, if necessary, from those who have repressively guarded the field in which this treasure has lain hidden for so long.

The ideal collection of writings about the New Testament, I propose, would not be a series of essays about the canonized text, but rather *a whole new set of Gospels,* with free and liberal interpretations of Jesus' ministry ringing out like really good jazz from the midsixties, ringing out with the kind of sublime poetry that we find in the King James Version of the Bible. With this in mind, we might see that the great ethical remarks of the late twentieth century emerge not only from the church, but also from where they are least likely to be. In John Coltrane's solos, in Mark Rothko's paintings, in doodlings of preschoolers, in the antigovernment and pro-choice politics of Soccer Moms, in the refugee camps of Eastern Europe or Africa or Central America, even in the writings of outspoken atheists like say, Michel Foucault: "Do not think that one has to be sad in order to be militant, even though the thing one is fighting is abominable."

The Gnostic writers of the first centuries of the Common Era presumed not that the gospels were the evidence on which they founded their faith, but that their faith was the evidence on which they founded their gospels. In their shadow canon, their parallel Christianity, language was hortatory, celebratory, even aleatory — it was a Joyful Noise — and upon this exhortation and celebration they pursued their faith, wherein joy itself, the joy of creation, was the finest evidence for the Divine.

In this spirit, then, we offer here a *de facto* reopening of the biblical canon. Or a step in the direction thereof. What would happen if we could entertain anew the spirit of political ferment of the first centuries after Jesus' death and allow interpretation to be as free and broad as it was then? What would happen? Trusting that the expanses of expression are the very dimensions of God him-, her-, or itself? What's to be feared in letting the faithful, or even those souls demonized as outsiders — doubters, unbelievers, and people of other faiths — think, at last, for themselves?

Jesus' Feet

Catherine Bowman

And when he had thus spoken, he showed them his *hands and* his *feet.*
LUKE 24:40

AND his feet. What were they like? Were they short and
stubby, long and angular, milky blue, tree-veined, delicate like
two rare fans, like two planks of stained and polished cherry,
gnarled, five toes like river rocks, spindly? Was the hair whiskered
or fleece? Were they calloused and cracked, caked with dirt and
still bleeding, or had they healed during his visit above? Were his
toenails calcified from the desert, pearled from the ocean, his
arches bowed, half-mooned, flat to the ground? Were they still
fragrant from the tears, the vinegar, Mary Magdalene's dark hair,
the costly oils imported from the Himalayas, the spikenard? Were
his feet slightly webbed from walking on water? After his time in
heaven did he like the way the earth felt on his toes?

JUST a few days before, he had washed the feet of the disciples
in this manner: One: *He riseth from supper.* Two: *And laid aside*

his garments. Three: *And took a towel.* Four: *And girded himself.*
Five: *He poureth water in a basin.* Six: *And began to wash the
disciples' feet.* Seven: *And to wipe them with the towel wherewith he
was girded.*

LAMENT, O Children of Israel, for this act of humility and
renunciation, this rite of purification, older than the pharaohs, a
loving and tender act of hospitality, soon to be renamed by the
church elders — *lavipedium.* In a public display once a year, one
poor man's feet are washed by a priest in full regalia. Stand
up and lament. From birthing to preparing for burial, we have
given the handling of our bodies over to the church and the
state.

AND he showed them his feet. And they saw not serum or syrup,
but two maps containing the oceans, and the land, and the
heavens. His foot-lines: the winds and the currents that coiled
around the world and all of the planets. So that their eyes opened
all at once: And they saw a woman's bound and wrapped feet;
they saw a bridegroom's feet washed in milk and vermillion; rows
of feet chained together, heat waves rising from the gravel at
dawn, the prisoners singing a prison work song; they saw two
velvet embroidered slippers.

THEY saw feet red with fatigue from walking the night district;
the feet of the shepherd crossing the valleys and tablelands; ten
thousand soldiers marching off to war; children sewing shoes for
children on the other side of the globe; a boxer bouncing on the

balls of his feet; feet mashing grapes; lovers rubbing their feet together under sheets.

FAR away an old blacksmith gathers up the footprint of a thief from the earth, wraps it in banana leaves and lays it on the coals of his forge.

FAR away a woman on a porch with arthritic feet watches her grandchild chase an adder through the reeds.

AND even farther now, a woman runs toward freedom with only the stars for guides, her feet bleeding from thorns and rock shards, the air full of bay leaf and pine. At the crossroads she sees the ghost of her grandfather, his feet backward as he steals her across the border.

WHEN he arrived that day on the road, he did not appear on a winged throne, garbed in amethyst vestments, on a cloud of roses and incense, in a whirlwind, on the shoulders of buffalo or angels, accompanied by mighty harps. Not swift as a comet or a bird or a thought. Not pulled in a barge or on a ball of fire. Unlike so many kings whose feet do not touch the ground, he showed up in town unannounced, walking on his own two feet. Hear and understand: Love does not make grand entrances but walks in unexpectedly on two human feet.

VERILY.

AND his feet, a couplet, a double harness, a duet, a duel, a movement in time, as the old man and woman dance on the hotel's rooftop garden on a balmy August night. The piano player sings "Caminito." *Since that day you left I have been so sad.*

THE couple now moving together in time, spelling out the secret code of a dance step, the thread that propels them through the labyrinth; all at once they are in flight, two hearts becoming one. As the body cannot be contained.

BLESSED be the vulnerable heel.

Blessed be the footstep, for it was our first drumbeat.

Blessed be the footprint and the bird track, for they were our first alphabet.

Blessed be the feet stained and tarnished by the dirt of the earth, by hard work, for the word *transcendent* comes to us from the Latin — to climb.

Blessed be the vital force of love, that rises up *from* the earth and enters and leaves the body through the feet.

STANDING there on that road they saw spirit transformed into matter. And we spend all our lives trying to transform matter back into spirit.

AND his feet. Two candles. Two mirrors. In thee, we rejoice. The rivers of hell start at his feet. Two caskets. Labia. Two twigs from a laurel broken in two. Two yeasty loaves of bread scented by the oven. Two ears of corn on the threshing floor. Two swine. Two crickets. Two vials of sticky sweets. The angular rays of the sun on water. Two reindeer across the tundra. The threads of rain and the spinning threads of summer light. Now, one atom splitting. His feet. Now, two immense talons. Now, the underbellies of two cows, where two bats suck milk in the moonlight, or the bellies split open, covered with flies, as two tigers feed in the shade of two thorn trees. In thee we rejoice. The last to leave the mother's body. And when we return to the earth, we are barefoot.

WHEN he came back after three days, he did not cast out devils, or heal lepers, cure with the weight of his shadow, or calm the storm. He showed them his feet. And then sat down to eat a piece of broiled fish, and a honeycomb.

Jesus Was a Convict

Kim Wozencraft

Two others also, who were criminals, were led away to be put to death with him. And when they came to the place which is called The Skull, there they crucified him, and the criminals, one on the right and one on the left. And Jesus said, "Father, forgive them, for they know not what they do." And they cast lots to divide his garments. And the people stood by, watching; but the rulers scoffed at him, saying, "He saved others; let him save himself, if he is the Christ of God, his Chosen One!"

The soldiers also mocked him, coming up and saying, "If you are the King of the Jews, save yourself!" There was also an inscription over him, "This is the King of the Jews."

One of the criminals who were hanged railed at him, saying, "Are you not the Christ? Save yourself and us!"

But the other rebuked him, saying, "Do you not fear God, since you are under the same sentence of condemnation? And indeed we justly; for we are receiving the due reward of our deeds, but this man has done nothing wrong." And he said, "Jesus, remember me when you come into your kingdom." And he said to him, "Truly, I say to you, today you will be with me in Paradise."

LUKE 23:32–43

JUDAS was the snitch in the government's case against Jesus, though his motive was vague. Others, perhaps only caught up in the spirit of the thing, gave false testimony against him. Soldiers carried out the sentence: they nailed him to the cross. His disciples had let him down every hour on the hour until Judas showed with the law — chief priests, scribes, and elders — and a crowd wielding swords and clubs. Then they abandoned him.

There is little I can point to, reading various accounts of Christ's execution in the Scriptures, to explain the sense I get that there was a party atmosphere surrounding the entire ordeal. Maybe it's the description of a clamorous crowd demanding that Pilate free Barabbas, an insurrectionist and murderer — a primitive Unabomber? — instead of Jesus. Or maybe it's the thought of soldiers rolling dice to see who got the garments that leaves me with the image of a drunken first lieutenant attempting to keep his balance as he stares up at a dead man on a cross while the sky above him is falling.

Every Sunday, from a time before I can remember until I was around eighteen years old, I knelt in a pew and was assaulted with a life-size statue of Christ on the cross hanging above the altar. Crowned with thorns. Blood dripping down one side of his face. A gash in the skin stretched tight over his agonized ribs, blood dripping; more blood trickling from the nail holes in his hands and feet. The weeks of Lent were a blessed relief, as they covered the statues with purple satin.

Perhaps the Catholic Church is onto something in its official condemnation of the death penalty. It has not strayed so far from its roots as to forget that its own savior was a victim of capital punishment. I may disagree vigorously with much of the church's doctrine, but I respect its stand on this issue.

That much of the Christian right falls into line and barks out "Yessir!" when the politicians chant *Three strikes, you're out!*, *Get tough on crime!*, and *Give us death instead of liberty!* leaves me wondering how they can fail to acknowledge that Jesus was a convict.

I know; he was betrayed. Most people who wind up in prison are. But the powers that were saw Jesus as guilty of insurrection, of treason, of attempting to overthrow the government. Serious charges, especially in the political tumult of the times. He was establishing a loyal following. They were scared of him.

I get mail from prisoners every day. Some are doing life with no parole for selling marijuana. Some are on death row, waiting for the state to kill them. When I think about death row prisoners, I am often reminded of Jesus hanging from the cross. His was the first execution I was exposed to.

I grew up not just Catholic, but Catholic in the Bible Belt. When I was in first or second grade, one of my friends turned on me suddenly and spat out, "My mother says I can't play with you anymore because you're Catholic and I'll go to hell."

When I was in high school, one of my closest friends confided to me one day that she couldn't visit my church because if you set foot in a Catholic church you would burn in hell. I think she was Episcopalian.

Meanwhile, my church was telling me that the Protestants were the ones who were missing the boat. And forget the Jews, the Buddhists, the Muslims. They were so far off base they weren't even talked about. It all seemed pretty crazy, but I was indoctrinated enough and scared enough that I said my Hail Marys and I genuflected before entering the pew; I ate fish on Fridays and hoped the Catholics had it together with God.

We were lucky to have some pretty hip folks in the parish who organized guitar masses and weekend retreats where seminary students came and sang, "I don't care if it rains or freezes, long as I got my plastic Jesus, riding on the dashboard of my car," and we learned the value of introspection, of meditation and prayer, and of fellowship. We liked the idea of Jesus throwing the money changers out of the temple. We liked that he wore his hair long. He was radical. And there were even intimations that God was — shhhh — *friendly.*

But by the time I was out of high school and could no longer be forced by Parental Decree to attend Mass regularly, I and most of my Catholic friends had been out of sync with the larger church for years. It treated women like property; it demanded unquestioning loyalty; it wanted us to get married and have lots of little Catholics to insure that the pews would be packed when the collection basket came around on Sundays. We found church policies empty and hypocritical.

Gradually, I fell away entirely, though I still think the Ten Commandments are a good set of general rules for living. To obey them out of fear, though, is limiting. Better we should look into our own hearts and discover that our knowledge of right and wrong has been there all along. Rules are obeyed, either out of fear or loyalty. Personal beliefs are felt, lived.

Now that I am a mother, I understand that except in cases where chemical imbalances wreak havoc on the brain, we humans come to this planet with an astonishing ability to love and be loved. The acts we call bad, and sometimes evil, are usually twisted attempts to guard against the loss of love. Contemporary American culture — yes, you *can* buy happiness — and those who advertise it have their role in perverting this innate human gentleness and compassion. And family circumstances, the luck of the draw, have their part as well. I visited a prison a few weeks ago and listened to men with life sentences talk to a group of very scared kids from the Bronx. The kids had been labeled PINS (persons in need of supervision). One of the convicts made a fist, shook it, and said, "How many of you, when you do something wrong, how many of you got parents who say, 'I'm gonna kick your ass?' " There were eleven kids there. Eleven hands went up. It's just the way things are.

Punishment, especially violent, extreme, or undeserved punishment, is effective in perverting or destroying the ability to love and be loved. Put a human in a cage for five, ten, twenty years; see what comes out.

And America seems to have grown big on punishment. The harsher the better. We cry to make prisons tougher, make sentences longer, kill more criminals. In a country that is overwhelmingly Christian, we have more people locked in prison than any nation in the world. We've brought back the death penalty. What's going on? What happened to compassion? What happened to forgiveness?

Here's Matthew on the topic:

> When the Son of man comes in his glory, and all the angels with him, then he will sit on his glorious throne.
>
> Before him will be gathered all the nations, and he will separate them one from another as a shepherd separates the sheep from the goats, and he will place the sheep at his right hand, but the goats at the left. Then the King will say to those at his right hand, 'Come, O blessed of my Father, inherit the kingdom prepared for you from the foundation of the world; for I was hungry and you gave me food, I was thirsty and you gave me drink, I was a stranger and you welcomed me, I was naked and you clothed me, I was sick and you visited me, I was in prison and you came to me.'

Aside from the goat bashing, this passage makes a great deal of sense to me. It's almost Eastern in orientation: all life is one. I feel a strong sense of community with humankind and believe that we mean well, usually. The criminal is a mess not because he's happy being that way, but because that's what he's been taught to be — by his family, by society, by an inept and corrupt crime-control establishment. Granted, there are some violence-prone individuals who must be kept locked up or they will rape or murder or kidnap or burn. But they are rare, and whether we can ever hope to understand their behavior, they, too, deserve our compassion. They make up a very small percentage of the people who are in prison these days. Most people in prison now are there because of the drug laws. Most people in prison are not violent. Most people in prison would like nothing more than to go back to their families and their jobs (if they were lucky enough to have one), and maybe try to get their property back from the government.

When I think about what would happen if Jesus showed up next Tuesday — not riding down from heaven on a cloud with trumpet fanfare blasting, but the way the Bible says he did it the first time, human born, I cannot help but feel certain that he'd wind up on death row, probably in Texas. This would, of course, be after he graduated from Harvard at thirteen and got fed into the media machine, made the rounds in TV land: *Oprah, Good Morning America,* maybe even *Geraldo. Larry King Live* would be a great venue for Jesus. We could call in. We could ask why there are tornadoes, why AIDS, why war. We could ask if the Western psychiatric establishment is part of the solution or part of the problem. And there would no doubt be numerous documentaries and a feature film, first rumored to be starring Tom Cruise, but in the end Brad Pitt would have to get the part.

Then everything would sour, and something would get whispered in a hallway somewhere in D.C. — *This guy is bigger than Michael Jackson and Madonna put together, and he's still gathering momentum* — and next thing you know, Jesus would be arrested. Betrayed again, no doubt. And instead of trying to post his bail, Hollywood — his production company, his agent, his lawyers, his publicist — would just bail out on him, as would most all of his other followers, except perhaps a loose, anonymous following on the Internet or maybe the odd militiaman who'd be willing to hole up in the name of Jesus and exchange fire with the feds.

The New Oxford Annotated Bible describes the political situation just before the birth of Christ thus:

> Growing political and religious divisions weakened the [Hasmonean] dynasty. The Sadducees, a politically minded aristocracy, were not averse to what they regarded as necessary concessions to the spirit of the times. The Pharisees, on the contrary, strove to maintain the separateness of the nation by refining upon the legal observances of the Mosaic code. Another religious sect, related to or identical with the Essenes . . . sought refuge in complete isolation from national life.

I suppose I would have been an Essene had I been around in those times. I can't see myself as an aristocrat, and I equate the Pharisees with the contemporary Christian right, which has become a political force dedicated to turning America into a police state. It does not surprise me that a secondary definition of *pharisee* is "hypocritically self-righteous and condemnatory." The same Christians who are willing, in the name of God, to torment a frightened and confused woman entering an abortion clinic will stand outside the prison walls and chant for the faceless executioner to get on with his business.

I know that much good is done at the hands of organized religions, Christianity among them. My first taste of poverty came when the CYO class I faithfully attended took Christmas turkeys and canned goods to families who lived in shacks in south Dallas. I was humbled and gratified by the experience. There were enjoyable times: Christmas caroling, the annual church picnic, the fund-raising fairs where the teenagers got to make and operate the haunted house. But every Sunday, there it was: the Agony of Christ. The Agony. The pain. The humiliation. The blood.

I cannot believe God is barbaric. The Old Testament stories, the statues, the legends depicted in stained-glass windows of churches across Europe, the history of God as an angry, vengeful, white-bearded male, are instructive only so far as giving a sense of how men have thought and acted throughout history.

I've spent years trying to shed my Catholicism, though I know that when my psyche is roiled, the sediment that clouds the waters is Catholic: the shame and guilt I learned at the hands of priests and nuns, each of them trying to do good according to their beliefs. I studied Catholicism prior to the most recent revision of the Baltimore Catechism. I can still feel the heavy blue paper cover and thin pages of the book from which we memorized questions and answers. And one of those questions, when put to me a few months ago by my four-year-old son, brought back the rote response I gave as a child in class.

"What is God?"

"God is love."

I know the answer is right, though I didn't understand it back when I was a scared-stiff little girl uttering memorized words and wondering when Sister Mary Helen was going to bean me with an eraser. I could tell by the look on my son's face that he didn't quite understand it, but that he was filing it away for further consideration.

He has asked about churches, too. I tell him they are places where people gather together to pray and to try to do good. That will have to do for now, because I can't explain why so many of the people who pray in those churches are ready to have the state kill convicts in the name of the people.

I understand the need for vengeance only too well. A man tried to take my life once, in the middle of the night, with a shotgun. I wanted to kill him. In fact, I wanted to torture him before killing him. I wanted him to suffer the way he made me suffer. When I see stories of kidnapping, rape, or murder in the news, when I see a grieving mother on the television screen and I think about how I would feel if someone harmed one of my children or my husband, I know I would want to get even. That, I suppose, is exactly the emotional chain politicians are trying to yank when they call for the death penalty. It's a quick, easy ticket to votes from anyone who feels the frustration of working day and night to make ends meet while watching the bad guys get away with murder.

My interpretation may well be flawed, but the biggest difference I see between the messages of the Old and New Testaments is that the New Testament replaces vengeance with forgiveness. All of the American Christians who are falling for the political doublespeak on crime control at the cost of losing their ability to feel compassion and forgiveness would do well to take a considered look at Luke's version of the Crucifixion.

Christ is on the cross, nails through his hands and feet, a thief hanging on either side of him. One thief makes fun of him. The other asks forgiveness. And, in what is the only instance in the entire New Testament of Christ actually promising heaven to anyone, Jesus says to the thief, "Truly, I say to you, today you will be with me in Paradise."

Of course, these days, we don't crucify. These days, executions are a bit more civilized. They should be. After all, it's Christians who are carrying them out.

Marvelous Revelation

Joanna Scott

WHEREFORE didst thou marvel?" the angel asks the prophet John as he contemplates one of the many fantastic visions that come to him on the island of Patmos. "I will tell thee the mystery of the woman, and of the beast that carrieth her, which hath the seven heads and ten horns," the angel promises, going on to explain in a typically elliptical fashion: "The beast that thou sawest was, and is not, and shall ascend out of the bottomless pit and go into perdition" (Rev. 17:7).

Was and is not and shall ascend. The Alpha and the Omega. The first and the last and the living one. These are a few of the powerful paradoxes that fill the Book of Revelation, paradoxes that are offered as solutions to the wondering prophet and that echo the central declaration of the New Testament: "I am he that liveth, and was dead." The reincarnation of Christ resolves the contradiction inherent in any fantasy of immortality, and paradox becomes cause for celebration. But in the last book of the New Testament, the only thoroughly apocalyptic book, paradoxical language takes on a new significance, since it is used in conjunction with a marvelous and titillating symbolism full of locusts with human faces, dragons and winged women and beasts with seven heads. How potent these images have proven through the centuries; how dangerous John's testimony becomes in the hands of zealots. It is the extraordinary punishments of the Book of Revelation that we remember most — and the paradoxes that we tend to ignore.

Apocalypse is synonymous with *revelation* and is derived from the Greek word *apokalypsis,* meaning an uncovering or laying bare. Of course, the term has taken on a lot of baggage over the centuries and is now inextricably associated with the four horsemen, the whore of Babylon, and divine vengeance. Apocalyptic rhetoric is the stuff of best-sellers that proclaim to reveal "the shocking truth" about the approaching end of history. While doomsday cults inspired by complex numerologies may spring up at any time, fin de siècles tend to stir apocalyptic fears. Now we're lucky enough — or not — to witness the final years of a millennium, and allusions to the punitive visions of the Book of Revelation seem to be everywhere. From apocalyptic preachers who claim to have pinpointed the date and location of Armageddon to politicians who warn us of a national moral crisis, language borrowed from Revelation is used to spice up rhetoric that would otherwise seem like mere nagging.

Borrowed language necessarily suffers from distortion, and Revelation's narrative, with its bizarre imagery, is especially susceptible. Contemporary doomsayers are like players in the children's game of telephone, changing the original message every time they pass it along. Those who declare that the battle of Armageddon will be fought in the year 2000 somewhere in Nebraska pass their fervor on to those who arm themselves in order to resist the coming New World Order, and they in turn pass their self-righteousness on to those who speculate publicly about the beast as they issue moral directives to their frightened audience. Phrase by phrase, John's figurative language is revised and diluted to suit particular uses until only key elements from the original text can be recognized. What begins as a prophet's feverish and deeply paradoxical testimony is turned into catch phrases like "moral crisis" and "end of history."

In this game of apocalyptic telephone, the first player is the preacher who makes a living — often a good living — preaching about the imminent apocalypse. He turns John's vision of the last days of worldly history into a description of millennial crisis. While the prophet John (whose relationship to the apostle John remains a contested point among biblical scholars) directs his message to "the seven churches of Asia," today's apocalyptic preacher extracts from Revelation a formula for contemporary society. "The world is now rushing toward an abyss of civil war, totalitarian world government, and the final devastation of nuclear, chemical, and biological warfare," one self-described "prophecy teacher" writes, claiming to have found in the Book of Revelation all the crucial information about what will happen upon the opening of the seventh seal — who will survive, when and where the battle of Armageddon will take place.

Apocalyptic preachers tend to bolster their zeal in two ways: they threaten nonbelievers with damnation, and they insist that their claims are entirely reasonable, weaving a web of logic around their illogical "truths." The Book of Revelation, despite its hallucinatory scenes, has its own sturdy web of logic. The use of numbers provides a forceful contrast to the colorful figurative language of the text — there are four horses, seven seals, seven angels; the first beast rules for forty-two months; the second beast has "a human number," six hundred and sixty-six. The numbers help us to define the symbols, to locate the allegory within a historical context (for instance, many scholars interpret the seven-headed beast as the Roman Empire and its heads as seven emperors). The numbers begin to make John's symbols more comprehensible, or at least they give a semblance of meaning to the strange vision.

Along with numbers, written language gives strength to John's testimony. He is told by Christ to "write the things which thou hast seen, and the things which are, and the things which shall be hereafter" (Rev. 1:19). At the Final Judgment, the dead are "judged out of those things which were written in the books" (Rev. 20:12). At one point, the angel commands John to take a scroll and eat it. Writing makes the images incontestable, or so the Book of Revelation seems to suggest (and to forestall tampering, the Book ends with a curse on anyone who dares to add to or take away from the text). What matters will be written down, and what is written will be read and judged.

Whether or not the startling events of the Book of Revelation were actually experienced by the prophet John as a vision, they are cleverly supported by precise locating details. And the successful apocalyptic preacher will imitate that precision. He will cite dates and numbers to prove that, as John announced nearly two thousand years ago, "the time is at hand." He will claim to draw on a combination of historical and scriptural documents. And he will point to recent events to prove that the end of worldly history is upon us.

The combination of comparative and precise language in John's testimony makes for a powerful cocktail, which is remixed, along with a good dose of hysteria, for consumption by a contemporary audience. But missing from this mix is paradox. At the heart of Revelation is a linguistic mystery — divinity is revealed only in an abstract paradox, Alpha and Omega, the beginning and the end. Opposites are joined in encompassing declarative phrases that are not backed up by concrete language. The central presence in the Book of Revelation defies literal and figurative description. Symbolism hedges the danger of idolatry by providing substitute images: the reincarnated Christ appears as the Lamb, Jerusalem as a bride, Rome as Babylon. But God, although made manifest to John at the end of his vision, is a paradox, indescribable. While the Holy Spirit is signaled in one passage with lightning and peals of thunder and is likened to jasper and "sardine stone" (Rev. 4:3–5), John never offers a defining image. God's identification, "I am Alpha and Omega," needs no supporting description — the paradox simply announces itself as "trustworthy and true" and so cannot be interpreted or applied to any particular thing. When John's vision threatens to become too precise, paradox interrupts the images, undoes the logic, and reminds us that Revelation is full of is-and-is-nots. Our comprehension depends upon obedient faith ("Worship God," we are told) rather than upon decipherment.

But still the self-appointed spokesmen for the apocalypse, stocked with images and metaphors, numbers and similes, argue that those of us living at the end of the twentieth century are destined to experience the tumult following the opening of the seventh seal. It is a seductive argument since it offers its audience the special privilege of significance: no prior crisis in human history will compare with the coming upheaval. Endings give meaning to disorderly life, and the apocalypse, the ending of endings, promises, at least in its essence, to answer all our questions. As Frank Kermode has written in his influential study of apocalyptic literature, *A Sense of an Ending,* "It is commonplace to talk about our historical situation as uniquely terrible and in a way privileged, a cardinal point of time." Now that we happen to be at the end of the second millennium A.D., the prophet-teachers have the calendar to wave in our faces.

And up spring the militant Aryans, who believe themselves to be the descendants of the lost tribes of the Biblical Israelites. White Christians, according to a doctrine called Christian Identity, are descended from Adam's son Seth (Cain's descendants, so Identity doctrine declares, are the Jews). In a fancy-stepping genealogy, Christian Identity traces the white race across the Caucasus Mountains to Scandinavia and western European countries, and across the ocean on the *Mayflower* to the true Promised Land. As the self-appointed chosen people of God, Identity followers are arming themselves for what the *Zion's Watchman* newsletter calls "the Consummation of an Age." Their militia mentality disguises aggression as preparation and defense. They find Revelation's symbols everywhere — in banking and commerce, in constitutional amendments, in the U.N. They build their "Aryan Halls," decorate their "Betsy Ross" flags with stars and swastikas, and stockpile weapons to protect themselves against the "alien tyranny evil" of other races. They seize on Revelation's most familiar symbols — especially the beast with its "human number," six hundred and sixty-six. They see the number everywhere, evidence that the beast has already arrived in the Promised Land.

"When revolutionary ideas are cast in an irresistible style," Fritz R. Stern writes in his study of German ideology, *The Politics of Cultural Despair,* "then seduction rather than comprehension is likely to follow." Armageddon is the ultimate revolution, and the Book of Revelation has proven itself a great seducer. The biblical scholar Leonard L. Thompson has described John's language as a stream that "flows into and out of images, figures, reiterations, recursions, contrasts and cumulations as whorls, vortices, and eddies. . . ." The metaphors and similes are wrapped around the concrete language, as in the description of events following the opening of the sixth seal: "Lo, there was a great earthquake; and the sun became black as sackcloth of hair, and the moon became as blood; And the stars of heaven fell unto the earth, even as a fig tree casteth her untimely figs, when she is shaken of a mighty wind. And the heaven departed as a scroll when it is rolled together; and every mountain and island were moved out of their places" (Rev. 6:12–14). The surprise of catastrophe is matched by the surprise of language, making our experience of the text more intimate. And just as with our dreams, such intimacy fools us into thinking that interpretation is an easy act. Revelation presents its images as symbolic masks, some of which are unmasked by John's angelic guide, who offers to "tell the mystery." In other passages, crowns and sickles, harps and fountains, linen and gold, and hundreds of other accessories are used to indicate divine stature. Evil is signified by dragons, beasts, and harlots. The Word of God rides in on a white horse. The allegorical nature of Revelation certainly begs for exegesis, but the text is by far the most mysterious book in the New Testament, and it protects its mystery, its carnival mask, from those who want to use it to describe their own historical moment.

Unfortunately, the strange images and warnings of Revelation are easily extracted from the complex whole. The beast lopes along Wall Street, nuclear weapons make real the possibility of total destruction, and the "lost tribes of Israel" prepare for the Great Tribulation in their isolated barracks. Move one place over in our apocalyptic telephone game and we get "a crisis of the spirit," or *decadence* in all its ugly splendor. The disintegration of morality "may be beyond the ken of politics, and beyond government solution," Pat Buchanan tells us in his smugly titled memoir, *Right from the Beginning,* so there's nothing to do but hunker down and make ourselves "the allies of our Judeo-Christian values."

It's important to note that there's a political element in all apocalyptic rhetoric. Responding to the tyranny of the Roman emperor Domitian (A.D. 81–96), John offers his testimony to bolster the struggling church. The author of Revelation was apparently an important church figure, steeped in the weighty language of the Old Testament. By closing the New Testament with a new version of the apocalypse, he was promising a kind of vindication that echoed Ezekiel and Isaiah and so was already familiar to the persecuted early Christians: all nations had been corrupted by Rome, or Babylon, and so all nations must suffer with the great city.

In the contemporary version of the apocalypse offered by the politician, mighty, doomed Babylon is vaguely associated with government. Buchanan blames everyone from the "practicing sodomite" to the Supreme Court (the "Imperial Judiciary," as he calls it) for our "moral disarmament and political paralysis." Although he outlines his fundamentalist agenda in some detail, his prediction is grim: the struggle to transform our society into a godly society will "likely provide us the only temporal reward we shall know." We are a doomed nation in Buchanan's opinion, but godly individuals can save themselves.

Through the centuries, people have directed Revelation's slippery narrative of retribution against all sorts of presumed evils — the pope, the Jews, the rich, the poor. For this reason D. H. Lawrence considered it the most hateful book in the Bible. He remained intrigued by what he called "the pagan vestiges" of

John's testimony, but he complained that much of the imagery cannot be imagined, citing as an example the four beasts "full of eyes before and behind" that sit "in the midst of the throne and round about the throne." "They can't be somewhere and somewhere else at the same time," Lawrence wrote in his own strange *Apocalypse,* blaming paradox for his exasperation.

Paradox is exasperating. It defies common sense and taunts us with abstractions, making the otherwise vivid images unimaginable. For this very reason, paradox plays an important role in Revelation. When we compare Revelation with Isaiah's "little Apocalypse," as it is sometimes called, we can gauge the effects of paradox more clearly, since this Old Testament version is not complicated by paradoxical language. The Lord is "mighty and strong, like a storm of hail, a destroying tempest" (Isa. 28:2). An "overwhelming scourge" will pass through, according to the "decree of destruction," and, prefiguring similar metaphors in Revelation, the heavens "shall be rolled together as a scroll" (Isa. 34:4). Isaiah's Apocalypse is by far more linguistically beautiful, full of powerful repetitions, an extraordinary accumulation of metaphors, and vivid imagery that, in contrast to much of Revelation's imagery, doesn't obscure its meanings. But while the terms of destruction and regeneration are more comprehensible in Isaiah, the verses lack the mystery of Revelation and so offer a less nightmarish prophecy.

The prophet John's testimony unfolds like a dream, with an odd, sometimes impenetrable but still forceful logic all its own. Whether we should read it as one man's account of a historical crisis around the time of the Emperor Domitian or as a vision of pending crisis remains the thorny exegetical question. The allegorical dimension of the text is obvious, but the allegory doesn't readily give up its secondary meaning.

So why not stick to the primary meaning? From Nostradamus to Ronald Reagan (who suggested that his generation might be the one to see the fulfillment of Revelation's prophecies), history has shown that the symbols are easily misconstrued. Rather than trying to connect the portents to exact dates, we might do better staying within the confines of the Bible and reading the Book of Revelation as a culminating vision — or dream — experienced by a man who was steeped in Scripture.

Revelation, though purporting to be a visual experience, often blurs its images with abstractions ("a golden cup full of abominations," for instance) and from the beginning privileges voice over vision (John hears the voice of Christ from behind him and only turns around after Christ's opening command). As a narrative of retribution, it seems an inappropriate addendum to the "good news" of the New Testament. But because of its great influence, I want to defend it against reduction and prefer to think of it as an illuminating response to the rest of the Bible, a devoted reader's dream — or vision.

I imagine John, exiled for his faith to the island of Patmos, standing beneath the open sky on a sweltering Sunday afternoon. A gull turns on the wing overhead, cries out, and in the silence that follows the old man hears "a voice like a trumpet." I imagine his rheumy eyes wide with wonder, though there is nothing before him, apparently, but a rocky hill sloping down to the sea, and nothing behind him but the wall of his stone hut. "Write the things which thou hast seen," the voice directs him. He experiences the total revelation in an instant, a flashed uncovering that in his memory contains the entirety of the Apocalypse, so that the vision, from the first trumpeting voice to the final promise, will take him months to record.

John's revelation is a *remembered* experience. Its strange images are dressed up in even stranger figures of speech that are drawn, in large part, from ancient and Judaic scripture. Whatever the solitary old man did see and hear on the island of Patmos is ornately decorated with metaphor and masked in allegory, and its primary message is "Worship God." At the end of the Bible, the faithful are left hoping for salvation. Revelation offers no prescription for change, no procedure that would help to prepare us for the end of history — indeed, it concludes with an order for acceptance and stasis: "He that is unjust, let him be unjust still; and he which is filthy, let him be filthy still; and he that is righteous, let him be righteous still; and he that is holy, let him be holy still" (Rev. 22:11). The point is not to decipher the allegory in order to pin down the date of the Final Judgment, but to be content with hope. The New Testament Apocalypse, full of paradox, ultimately eludes our imagination; imaginable versions are useless distortions. For John, sitting alone on his island beneath a brilliant blue sky, breathing in the fragrance of a nearby eucalyptus, his fierce faith was momentarily rewarded with aural and visual correlatives. For the rest of us, faith is blind.

A Love Supreme

Madison Smartt Bell

I HAVE a peculiarly scrambled memory of my first encounter with 1 Corinthians 13; it was in my elementary school auditorium, which also doubled as gym. Certain particulars remain very vivid — it must have been late afternoon, because of the slanting, reddening light that spread on the high-gloss floorboards like a stain. I remember the indefinable institutional odor of trapped air, and the squeaking of the gray metal folding chairs we all sat in, and the dust motes that swirled in bars of sunlight around the curtains on the stage. On the stage, someone was reading the words of Saint Paul.

> Though I speak with the tongues of men and of angels, and have not charity, I am become as sounding brass, or a tinkling cymbal.
>
> And though I have the gift of prophecy, and understand all mysteries, and all knowledge, so that I could remove mountains, and have not charity, I am nothing.

My memory provides the image of one of my own classmates, a lean little girl with long dark hair and sharp features, who was, in a hard-bitten way, sort of beautiful. I see her standing near the lip of the stage, reading or reciting the verses, but I can't imagine why she was doing this. It seems unlikely that she would have been. Was it some exercise in elocution? or memorization? But in that case why would it happen in front of the whole assembly? And at any rate the text seems rather improbable for such an exercise. Still, I can see her standing there, only a little awkwardly, saying the words in a rote, singsongy fashion, which made it clear that she didn't understand them much better than I did.

> And though I bestow all my goods to feed the poor, and though I give my body to be burned, and have not charity, it profiteth me nothing.

This is the verse that really threw me, there in the grade school auditorium — because what did charity mean if not giving stuff to the poor? I had no sense of a larger definition or a larger implication. I thought charity meant giving things to beggars. I had no direct experience with any beggars at that time, however, and my only involvement with charity as I understood it involved turning in canned corn for food drives, or something of that sort.

> Charity suffereth long, and is kind; charity envieth not; charity vaunteth not itself, is not puffed up.

This sounded to me more like humility — of which I did have some conception.

> Doth not behave itself unseemly, seeketh not her own, is not easily provoked, thinketh no evil;
> Rejoiceth not in iniquity, but rejoiceth in the truth;

Beareth all things, believeth all things, hopeth all things, endureth all things.

The definition, or description, didn't help my confusion much. Most of the above-listed virtues had been recommended to me somewhere before, but how did all these virtues get under the umbrella of charity, which (so far as I understood) meant giving stuff to beggars?

Charity never faileth: but whether there be prophecies, they shall fail; whether they be tongues, they shall cease, whether there be knowledge, it shall vanish away.

For we know in part, and we prophesy in part.

But when that which is perfect is come, then that which is in part shall be done away.

When I was a child, I spake as a child, I understood as a child, I thought as a child: but when I became a man, I put away childish things.

For now we see through a glass, darkly; but then face to face: now I know in part; but then shall I know even as also I am known.

How did that little girl, my classmate, ever get those words to come out of her mouth? Maybe she didn't — I have remembered it wrong. It must have been some visiting preacher. But still it is her whom I see with my mind's eye.

And during this passage, as the text moved into vatic mode, I myself shifted into a state of relatively contented bewilderment. Verses 8 through 12 of 1 Corinthians 13 are somewhat difficult matter even for adults, I would still contend, and there was no hope that I could cogitate my way through them way back then.

But I was content to hear without understanding. I think many people who grew up *listening* to the King James Bible may have had similar experiences. Because of its power as poetry, the King James translation makes its first and most vivid impression on the ear; from the force of its arrangement of pure sounds (sometimes regardless of their sense), it obtains its first authority. It imprints itself on the mind as an auditory pattern that may not become fully intelligible until long afterward. . . . At which time one may also feel a spooky sense of familiarity, of déjà vu.

> And now abideth faith, hope, charity, these three, but the greatest of these is charity.

At the closing verse, I started cogitating again. This bit didn't make any sense to me either. Because now that faith had been mentioned, it struck me that the virtues listed in verses 4 through 7 were far more characteristic of faith than of charity, according to my understanding of the two. I thought faith was the big magical quality that could somehow transform everything it contacted — a virtue that absorbed all the others. Indeed, I would have assumed that the virtues enumerated in the concluding verse of the chapter were listed in descending rather than ascending order of importance. First of all you were supposed to believe, and next (consequent to your belief) you were supposed to hope for salvation, and then (incidentally and by the way) you were supposed to try to be nice to the people around you (because that was a conventional and thus-to-be-taken-for-granted Christian virtue). Hadn't the chapter from 1 Corinthians turned that hierarchy upside down?

I left the auditorium scratching my head, and the itch persisted, perhaps permanently, though I was not always aware of it.

*　　*　　*

A S for the occasions of my subsequent brushes with 1 Corinthians 13, I remember them much less vividly and distinctly than that first one. But somewhere along the line I was made acquainted with the distinctions between different kinds of love that figure in Christianity: *eros, agape,* and *caritas.* Eros, romantic or sexual love, was far and away the most familiar and is the most frequently deployed in modern society. God's love for mankind was agape, further defined by analogy to a mother's love for her children. As mother love, agape is still (one hopes) familiar to the majority, but as God's love I suspect it has evolved into a theological abstraction. *Caritas,* translated as "charity" in the KJV, was yet another thing, a sort of fellow feeling, a love that didn't want anything for itself, a love without possessiveness and divorced from desire. I no longer recall where I came by these definitions, or even if they are accurate, though they are still more or less the definitions I use for my own orientation.

Caritas, charity, seemed more difficult and distant a concept even than agape because one could not approach it very conveniently with analogies. But I saw that it was distinct and somehow important, and therefore I sort of resented it when, as a high school and college student, I began to run into translations of 1 Corinthians 13 that substituted "love" for "charity." At first glance this usage might seem to be superior, because after all, a general kind of love is intended, rather than the specific and narrow quality of generosity to the poor. And indeed, the substitution of "love" in this context eliminates the confusion that I underwent as a child and afterward — so much so that one might read through the passage without really having to think about it, without ever being stopped short. But "love" is an insufficiently precise term for the situation, and its use endows the whole passage with a sort of sentimentality that I doubt Saint Paul ever intended. I imagine Saint Paul would have preferred that we be stopped short and arrested, temporarily, in a state of confusion.

W E do not at present live in an age of faith. When I say "we," I don't mean those who are borne up by the rising tides of fundamentalism in both Christianity and Islam. I mean the community of "secular humanists" to which I belong by virtue of my education. And if you are taking the trouble to read this essay, your education was probably sufficiently similar to mine. To those thus educated, faith is apt to become a rather difficult problem, something one knows better how to wish for than achieve. As for hope, well, most of us have grown up in the shadow of a doomsday mentality produced by the possibility of nuclear armageddon, and if this threat has retreated a little with the end of the Cold War, the possibility of an environmental doomsday seems more than adequate to fill the gap. If our hopes in this world are thus problematic, our hopes for the next also become difficult to the extent that hope depends on faith. What, then, of charity?

W H E N I was a little more grown up, I became a fiction writer and wrote a number of novels that now appear to me to be in one way or another accounts of different spiritual pilgrimages. I did not see them that way while I was writing them; they were just stories I thought were interesting enough to try to tell. But in retrospect I see that each has near enough to its center some sort of experiment with religion or philosophy or both: Islam, Sufism, Santeria, Russian Orthodox Christianity, French existentialism, Christian existentialism as espoused by Kierkegaard, and so on. After writing this series of books I wrote another, *Soldier's*

Joy, whose conscious intentions were explicitly political. I wanted to write a book about resistance to racism in the rural South, where I was raised. This was a novel without any deliberate religious mission, but all the same, an itinerant preacher did wander into it somehow, so that the following conversation took place:

> Laidlaw jerked his head back toward the truck, where Ratman was still circling around the area of the tailgate. "I've heard it told there ain't no God," he said.
>
> "No doubt you have," Brother Jacob said. "That's what the fool said in his heart."
>
> Laidlaw looked him back in the eye. "Do you yourself truly believe?"
>
> "Well you may ask." The preacher's voice went suddenly low. "Maybe He's left us. Maybe He's just gone off, like some claim it. Don't make no difference anyway."
>
> "What's that you say?" It was Raschid's voice asking the question, but the preacher, though he hadn't moved any nearer, now seemed to be talking only in Laidlaw's ear. And Laidlaw had the perplexing suspicion that no matter what use he'd planned to make of it the preacher had meant what he was saying all along.
>
> "The point is, what did He do when He was with us? He loved people, that's what He did. Only not with a fool's blind love, the way some misremember it now. He loved out of the full under-standing. He'd see down through every darkest turn of your soul, know you better than you knew yourself, and love you still in spite of all. Saint Paul called that charity. And charity is God among us, even to this day. And that's what I believe."

This peroration of course amounts to an interpretation of verses 9 through 12 of 1 Corinthians 13. *Caritas* requires an omniscient knowledge of whoever is to be loved. The definition of *caritas* involves the idea of loving people not just for the good things about them but for (and despite) *everything* they have about them for good or ill. And yet we are not given to know one another so completely on this earth, *for we know in part, and we prophesy in part.*

Of the four difficult verses 9 through 12, the twelfth is perhaps the most opaque, harnessing a puzzling image in the first half to a syntactical contortion in the second half. *For now we see through a glass darkly, but then face to face* is a line that looks forward to a moment of revelation when the veils that partially conceal us from one another will be torn away — when it will be given to us to know one another wholly. *Now I know in part; but then shall I know even as also I am known* — what that twisted passive first suggests is the omniscience of God, which the striving soul experiences as its object. Secondly comes the thought that under the light of revelation, souls may so reveal themselves to one another. *Caritas,* charitable love in the Pauline sense, depends on complete and limitless knowledge of others, but such knowledge is a divine attribute, not a human one.

The implications for a faithless age are interesting. Although an unskeptical belief that God exists may be difficult in our time, the correct and sincere practice of charity forces us to behave as if he did. *Faith, hope, charity, these three; but the greatest of these is charity.*

A PILGRIMAGE requires a pilgrim: an anxious individual striving soul with its own particular complex of needs and ambitions and fears and desires. Last summer I made a pilgrimage of my own, to Haiti, a country I had spent ten years reading and thinking about but had never before seen in the flesh. In Haiti almost every tap-tap bus is festooned with Catholic imagery and crowned with some such slogan as *Christ Capable,* but Christianity has evolved quite a long way from the forms introduced by the Spanish and the French. Many islands in the Caribbean practice versions of Christianity that have syncretized with African beliefs, but because Haiti has been so thoroughly isolated for such a long time, the African strain in the Haitian religion, *vaudou,* is unusually strong and pure.

Immortality in *vaudou* is simple and concrete; dead souls do not leave the world but remain, translated into a vast reservoir of spiritual force known in aggregate as *Les Morts et Les Mystères.* From this reservoir are formed the *loa,* a pantheon of deities that bears an archetypal resemblance to the Greek and the Roman pantheons, and indeed to most other mythological assemblies of gods. But in Haiti, the *loa* commune with their believers on a very regular basis; they are as familiar as members of the family, and certainly as influential.

Faith is not problematically abstract for *vaudou* believers; they have no difficulty in reaching their gods. A regular part of *vaudou* observance involves eradicating individual consciousness from the mind so that the body can be occupied — possessed — by the particular *loa* who is served by the believer. The gods of *vaudou* are fully manifest in the world of the living, and they do not only show their hinder parts, as God consented to show himself to Moses however many thousand years ago. For reasons like these, *vaudou* strikes me as the most vital religion I know of on earth, but it does not seem open for me to adopt; the culture and history I come from are too alien . . . perhaps. In Haiti, I felt a little like someone with his face pressed to a wall of glass, pining for unreachable treasures beyond it.

When I traveled in Haiti, I saw, or thought I saw, that the

individual striving self was far less important in Haitian experience than in American life, and that the sense of community was far more natural and more powerful for Haitians than it is for us. Perhaps there is something about the *vaudou* believer's regular and radical self-abnegation that puts the individual self in a less important place than it occupies with us, and that opens the self more fully to forming bonds with others. Haitians seem to feel an organic sense of continuity with their community that would seem very strange to most citizens of the First World. This phenomenon permeates many levels of Haitian life; for instance, the word for "we" in Haitian creole is the same as the word for "you."

In Port-au-Prince I went to a performance by a band called Boukman Eksperyans; this group is part of a larger musical movement heavily influenced by *vaudou* rhythms, and their concerts double as religious rites. The first phase of the performance didn't seem to go well; the band members broke off rather abruptly and retired to form a prayer circle, which for some reason they invited me to join. We all joined hands, and they began to chant; presently I understood that they were reciting the Lord's Prayer in creole. This recognition moved me very powerfully, gave me a feeling of rootedness among them that I would not have thought possible. At the moment that the prayer ended and our hands disconnected, I happened to catch sight of myself in a small makeup mirror just barely large enough to frame my face; it was the only reflective surface in the room. I felt shock and an awful feeling of turbulence and (while exchanging embraces with all the others in a variation of the kiss of peace) I began crying and for some time could not stop.

At first I thought my reaction had to do with race. In fact I had not recognized myself in the mirror at first glance; my first thought was *A white person — what is he doing here?* And after the recognition, a white person did seem a horribly inappropriate thing to have to be.

But skin is a minor aspect of the shell of ourselves. Before I went to Haiti I had spent most of my adult life inventing stories about individual pilgrims and the goals of their pilgrimages. In Haiti I saw (or thought I saw) that the individual self is a prison. I was reprieved from my self for a time, but after my return to the States the effect wore off (slowly and rather painfully) until I lapsed back into my former confinement.

What a dark glass that was, after all! Now, a year past my first visit to Haiti but only a few days away from my next, I think that I recoiled so from my image in the mirror because it flung me back into myself. When a glass is perfectly transparent it does not reflect at all; it leaves one openly face-to-face with those on the other side. If the self is a prison, then maybe charity is the key that can open the door. Or, as the Sufi poet Rumi wrote, "You become bewildered; then suddenly Love comes saying, 'I will deliver you this instant from yourself.' "

Within and Without

Stephen Westfall

*And when he was demanded of the Pharisee when the kingdom of God
should come, he answered them and said, The kingdom of God cometh not with
observation:*
    *Neither shall they say, Lo here! or, lo there! for behold, the kingdom of God
is within you.*

LUKE 17:20–21,

KING JAMES VERSION

*And I say unto you, That many will come from the east and west, and shall
sit down with Abraham, and Isaac, and Jacob, in the kingdom of heaven.*

MATTHEW 8:11 / LUKE 13:29

I

Just imagine. You've been taught that
a man's outward wealth is a sign of his favor in the eyes of God,
that righteousness is something achieved through pious adher-
ence to the letter of the law of Moses and the prophets, that the
Messiah is coming to set your suffering and quarrelsome nation

first at God's table in heaven and here on earth. After years of effort to achieve and maintain wealth, family, position, *and* piety (at the cost of a tremendous inner struggle to rein in your most rebellious impulses and do the right thing), after all of that, the son of God walks into your village looking for prostitutes, tax collectors, beggars, the lame and sick. How would you feel? Imagine, for a moment, that all your exertions to make something of your life, to make God proud of you, have left you desirous of a little recognition. Maybe just a quick stop by the house for some tea and dates. But you're passed over; the so-called Messiah blows through to the outskirts, where he begins to teach the rabble. Personally, I'd go nuts. Nobody's going to whip the Romans with those losers.

On the the other hand, if it were true that the kingdom of heaven is within, and we dwelt there with awareness, we might feel quite differently. Overthrowing Roman rule might be beside the point. Our wealth would be become a vehicle for actions born of our awareness. Our righteousness would be laid at the feet of humility. We could find ourselves eagerly among the ragged crowd that we had earlier scorned. Perhaps most profoundly, the crippling burden of our self-consciousness would have lifted, a burden whose load we hadn't noticed until it lightened. This self-consciousness, far from being connected to our inner kingdom, is the very force propelling our external search and our deferral. It is what prevents us from "just being with the people," as I once heard it put.

All the spiritual traditions describe an inner realm of consciousness whose doors open to contemplative practice. Various Yogis refer to the seat of this inner realm as the "Self," not to be confused with the lowercase self that dominates the concerns of the ego. Buddhist traditions term this state "Buddha-mind" or "Buddha-nature." Here, "mind" includes the knowledge and intimations of the heart. I think this is something of what Jesus is offering us when he speaks of "the kingdom of heaven." The implications of what he said completely overturned the prevailing view around the ancient world. In that world, wealth and position by birth were not only the measure of one's pull with the Divine, they were the almost necessary prerequisites for the pursuit of a transformative consciousness. Even the Buddha had worked his way up a karmic food chain over countless lifetimes, so that in his final incarnation he was a prince, with the leisure and powers of command to indulge his thirst for the sacred. To believe in the inner kingdom proclaimed by Jesus is to accept that God has already granted his Grace, that it is available to anyone at any time because it already resides in everyone. It cannot be conferred, nor can it be abolished by decree. Neither the state nor the family has power over it. In this sense, the apprehension by an individual of the kingdom of heaven precedes any broader social intention, any question of justice.

A bastard son of a carpenter's wife unveils a source of creative tranformation of everyday life that the swineherd, tax collector, and beggar possess in equal measure to emperors, generals, and high priests. Even members of other, hated tribes and, perhaps, followers of other faiths are invited to the feast. Jesus represents the end of the ancient world because he overthrows the moral laws that had established its ethics and social hierarchies. I love who Jesus is because his low rank, his sensuality, his physical suffering and momentary faltering of faith on the cross, bring him nearer to me. In the person of Jesus, God gets down here with us and gets his hands dirty. He reaches out to me, "the poor in spirit."

II

My own spiritual rebirth was initiated several years ago, when I had come to a place where my own resources could not carry me an inch farther. I was heartbroken, pissed off, a physical wreck, preoccupied with loss, and finally frightened enough to ask for help. I can't be sure whether fear was the sole motivator of my sudden willingness or if there was a simultaneous surge of creativity from within that took surrender as its gesture. I do know that I nearly instantaneously felt a flood of peace. Part of what I had held to tightly as my identity died in that moment and in its wake left a spaciousness for contemplation and action unobstructed by the fears and rationalizations that had been there moments before. I don't recall thinking about Jesus, or a Christian redemption. Maybe I prayed the foxhole prayer, "God, get me out of this," and perhaps a residual image of the compassionate poster Jesus from Episcopalian Sunday school flashed in my mind. I was, however, "visited" by a voice (not the historical Jesus', it was feminine!) that comforted me and opened a door of perception for an instant. I believe the voice, the peace, the willingness, the surrender, the spaciousness, and the creative insight were together one thought, an "illumination." I also believe that this thought represented not so much a discrete insight as it did a glancing contact with a creative continuance unfolding in my body and around my conscious mind whether I choose to be aware of it or not.

During the first years that followed this moment of crisis and brief breakthrough, I devoted myself primarily to the immediate therapy I needed to physically and psychically mend. I found that my reading turned from fiction and theory to psychology. I was never previously able to get very far with psychology texts, but now I experienced an empathetic response to reading Winnicott, Sullivan, Nuemann, M. Esther Harding, and James Hillman. Though they all had different areas of concern, I was impressed by the healing power of metaphor in their writings overall and the emphasis on dreams in the work of the latter three authors. I began to have emotional resonance with the metaphoric model of the journey as it applies to the development of consciousness in a life span. Sometimes the journey covers a lot of mileage underground, so to speak. I started keeping a dream journal and was surprised by the beauty, metaphoric complexity, emotional richness, and occasionally painful clairvoyance of my dream life.

In the summer of 1993 I had a dream in which I went to a service at the Episcopal church down the road from Bard College, where I was teaching painting in a summer residency program for graduate students in the creative arts. It was Sunday morning, and I hadn't been to a Sunday service in years, but, because of the dream, I resolved to attend that very morning. I went and nothing happened. Beyond nothing. The regular priest was out of town, and instead of the Eucharist, the service was the comparatively perfunctory Morning Prayer. The hymns seemed drier than ever, and the congregation was sparse. The language of the revised Book of Common Prayer had been reduced from the aristocratically archaic cadences of the original to the near flatness of everyday speech. I didn't stay for coffee, but instead left disappointed, unaware that when I had walked in with expectations of illumination I had left the kingdom of heaven at the door. I couldn't just be with the people.

That winter I was becoming increasingly anxious to learn meditation. I could pray like nobody's business, but because my attention span is gnatlike (this may insult the gnat), I was utterly unable to meditate. I couldn't rise above or sink below the level of chatter in my head. Two friends intervened. The first gave me a copy of Stephen Levine's book *A Gradual Awakening,* which provides a gentle entry into meditation practice with a sympathetic address to the noisy-headed, heartbroken, and fearful. The second friend pointed out that almost all serious work with meditation begins with a teacher, booked me into a New Year's retreat at an upstate ashram, and drove there with me.

At the ashram I was confronted by my own sense of embarrassment. There were two or three thousand devotees, and I couldn't believe that I was stuck up there for three days admidst this throng. Every individual I met was perfectly lovely, alert, and fully capable of irony. But when I beheld the masses in a lunch line or in the coatroom, I couldn't shake the feeling that they were zombies, pod people. Upon reflection, I realize that I would have felt this way if I had been on an Episcopalian retreat, or at any gathering inspired by stated spiritual goals. I don't feel this way at sporting events or concerts, even though mass idolatry is as present at those events as it is anywhere.

In spite of my anxiety and ambivalence, I "got" some initiate level of meditation right away. One of the swamis guided us through a warm-up meditation and asked us not to try and stop our thinking but simply to be aware of it and gently bring our attention back to our breath and the mantra. I felt the burden of trying too hard to stop thinking lift. The guru herself proved to be an immensely charismatic being and quite funny in her talks. I was too abashed to say anything to her when I was presented for an introduction, but she touched the open palm of my hand, and in that moment I felt the openness of the invitation of the spirit. I was free to keep primary allegiance to my other spiritual paths, and I would always be welcome here. In that moment I was also freed to do some spontaneous service. I went to the cafeteria kitchen and joyously joined other volunteers in helping clean up after the evening meal.

I I I

The Jungian analyst and Episcopal priest John Sanford points out in his book *The Kingdom Within* that the phrase from Luke that he takes as his book's title has been rendered differently in recent editions of the Bible, such as the Revised Standard Edition:

The passage from Luke 17:21 would seem to clearly refer to the kingdom as an inner reality, except for the confusion regarding the Greek preposition rendered in this King James translation "within." The preposition in question can also mean "among" and has been so translated by almost all the modern translators of the Bible in preference to "within." This choice of translation derives from the extroverted attitude of our time, which finds it hard to conceive that anything worthwhile could be within us. In the early Church, however, this preposition was invariably translated into the Latin equivalent of "within." Being closer to Jesus' time, the Fathers were also closer to his spirit and knew of the reality of the inner world. There is a sense in which the kingdom of heaven is both within ourselves and outside ourselves and among us and other people. The ambiguity of the Greek preposition *entos* is probably deliberate.

He attributes this shift in meaning to the gradual abandonment by organized religion in the West of an emphasis on the inner life of the individual soul, "the eye of the heart," as Saint Augustine described it. Sanford writes:

> The soul today is an orphan. . . . Philosophy, her father, long ago decided she did not exist and cast her aside. He hardly noticed that in so doing he turned away from wisdom and became confined to the narrow realm of semantics and semiotics. The Church, her mother, fell unwittingly into the clutches of the extroverted, rationalistic materialism of our times and so also abandoned the soul; she did not notice that in losing the soul she lost her ability to relate the individual to God.

This abandonment was set in motion during the Enlightenment by the shift in intellectual discourse to an emphasis on quantifiable knowledge. The church spent futile energy upholding the tenets of the Bible as the arbiter of the physical laws of the universe. The absurd spectacle of contemporary Creationism passing itself off as science is but a poignant example of the persistence of what the brilliant consciousness theorist Ken Wilber gently terms a "category error," where specialists in particular domains of experience and knowledge attempt to pass judgment and exert influence on other domains by engaging systems of verification that are adequate only within their own areas.

In his book *Eye to Eye* Wilber outlines three principal cultural domains — science, philosophy, and religion — and argues that each has its own way of seeing, respectively: physical/empirical, mental/rational, and transcendental (or spiritual)/contemplative. While their borders of knowledge may necessarily remain in dispute, the core of each domain, each "eye," remains vast and relatively autonomous. Each has its own system of verification, which posits a set of instructions ("If you want to know this, do this"), which in turn generates a body of knowledge or experience, out of which is formed a consensus with others engaged in the same practices. According to Wilber, "This constitutes a communal or consensual proof of *true seeing*." Just as someone who has refused to study geometry has no business declaring geometric proofs invalid, one who has not engaged in contemplative practices cannot be a reliable authority on the validity of contemplative experience. There is, however, overwhelming consensus among those from every spiritual tradition who do engage in such practices about the authenticity and general nature of their experiences. "The kingdom of heaven is at hand," says Jesus, meaning literally right here and now.

I V

Jesus bursts into the consciousness of the ancient world with the news of a creative, loving God's immediate, universal presence, but there is little indication of an intention to start a new religion. His God is the God of Abraham and Isaac. And nowhere in the Gospels is there any indication of his intention to exclude those who practice other traditions from direct encounter with the spirit. Thus, his statement to the believing centurion from Matthew 8:11, which goes on in the next verse, mysteriously, "But the children of the kingdom shall be cast out into outer darkness; there shall be weeping and gnashing of teeth." I detect enormous compassion verging on sorrow in this passage. We do conduct ourselves amid suffering and repression and, inevitably, are ourselves sometimes the cause. Jesus' mission is *to* the excluded, the powerless, the shamed, the dejected and rejecting. At the agonizing end of his mortal journey he will be one with them, even to the point of the trembling of his mortal faith.

Perhaps because of the urgency of his message, he has little to say about contemplative method. His teaching appears to emphasize sudden illumination, *epiphany*, through parable, judicious deployment of miracles, right action, and extensive instruction on forgiveness (Jesus has more useful things to say about the difficulty and necessity of forgiveness than any teacher before him). He teaches a charitable humility, grounded in joy over the creative abundance of the spirit's outreach. Nevertheless, *what* is illuminated is *within* the individual. It has always been present, waiting, as it were, for its illumination. And it must be illuminated because it cannot be described in either physical or rational terms. Even the term "illumination" cannot be taken literally. And for us to be so moved by second- and third-hand accounts of Jesus' actions and speech probably requires some form of contemplation.

There does appear to be a considerable and growing body of contemporary literature on the contemplative methods of various Buddhist, Vedic, and Sufi traditions. Post-Enlightenment Christian literature is as comparatively spotty on practical, compassionate instruction as it is long on testimony, argument, and scholarly exegesis. This absence will no doubt be addressed in the next few years, partly through increased dialogue with other faiths. In the meantime, I will take Jesus' statement from Matthew 8:11 as an open invitation to come to the table of the kingdom of heaven however we can. And here is one of the realizations of the inner kingdom itself: I cannot experience the kingdom of heaven within me and remain blind to its innateness within you. If I deny or scorn you, I do it to myself. *Within* is hereby brought into alignment with *among*, and I am freed to be myself among every other beautiful one.

"Was" in John

Jim Lewis

1 In the beginning was the Word, and the Word was with God, and the Word was God.

2 The same was in the beginning with God.

3 All things were made by him; and without him was not any thing made that was made.

4 In him was life; and the life was the light of men.

5 And the light shineth in darkness; and the darkness comprehended it not.

6 There was a man sent from God, whose name was John.

7 The same came for a witness, to bear witness of the Light, that all men through him might believe.

8 He was not that Light, but was sent to bear witness of that Light.

9 That was the true Light, which lighteth every man that cometh into the world.

10 He was in the world, and the world was made by him, and the world knew him not.

11 He came unto his own, and his own received him not.

12 But as many as received him, to them gave he power to become the sons of God, even to them that believe on his name:

13 Which were born, not of blood, nor of the will of the flesh, nor of the will of man, but of God.

14 And the Word was made flesh, and dwelt among us, (and we beheld his glory, the glory as of the only begotten of the Father,) full of grace and truth.

15 John bare witness of him, and cried, saying, This was he of whom I spake, He that cometh after me is preferred before me: for he was before me.

16 And of his fulness have all we received, and grace for grace.

17 For the law was given by Moses, but grace and truth came by Jesus Christ.

18 No man hath seen God at any time, the only begotten Son, which is in the bosom of the Father, he hath declared him.

JOHN 1:1–18

FROM a certain perspective the very idea of a New Testament is somewhat odd — as, consequently, is the idea of an Old Testament. For Jews, even delinquent ones like myself, there's only one book of religious law, which for the sake of convenience we can call the Hebrew Bible, and the body of writings produced by the followers of Christ is a strange addition, remarkable in its own way, but as a kind of powerful curiosity. I would imagine mainstream Christians feel much the same about the Koran, or the Book of Mormon; they're examples of that distant and scarcely comprehensible event that I tend to think of as Someone Else's Revelation, a phenomenon that, like Someone Else's Love Affair, calls forth the very ambivalence about different lives that it's designed to address. So while I read the Hebrew Bible as a child (and read it as a child does: fitfully and reluctantly), I knew the New Testament only by hearsay; my first encounter with it as a complete work came in graduate school, when it was a required part of a syllabus that I happened to be teaching.

But of course I knew it was there; I'd absorbed some of the stories, I recognized many of Jesus' lines. More importantly, I *felt* it, because to be a Jew is to perceive oneself, on some level at least, as being surrounded by Christianity, encompassed by it, enveloped in it. I mean this quite literally, but I mean it more than literally, too, for the original goal of the authors of the Gospels — as I discovered when I finally sat down to read them — was precisely to surround Judaism by taking up Jewish law, history, and poetry and transfiguring them. The New Testament, to me, is the means by which Judaism was surrounded, and to the extent that it succeeds, Christianity itself succeeds.

So be it: culture is a beast ruled only by its appetite; it devours what it will, and I've always assumed that the best response is the obvious one: to maintain one's own cultural life in whatever form one has the will and the means to do so. Still, I've occasionally found it frustrating. I remember, by way of pointed example, a reviewer of my first novel for the *Los Angeles Times* who somehow found the book suffused with Christian symbolism, a hypothesis she backed up by citing some rather oblique references she'd found in its pages to the Song of Solomon. She was right about the references, but wrong about their intended provenance, for I've always thought of the Song as a Jewish poem, composed some three or four centuries before the birth of Christ by people who had no inkling of the teachings he would pass down and no particular fondness for symbolism as a poetic tactic.

My point is not just that it was all too easy for the woman to assume that I was a Christian writer, hence that I treated the Song as a Christian poem, but that in doing so she necessarily failed to understand the book — and not just by misinterpreting its content, but by misapprehending its style. Because Christian writing is different from Jewish writing; it represents the world differently, using different kinds of figuration, a different syntax, different transitions; it has a different purpose, and it manifests a different ethic. So a single piece of writing can take on one cast or another, depending upon how it's read.

We read according to presumption, and at the risk of being crude to the point of inanity, I would suggest that the Christian way with poetic language is essentially symbolic: it traffics in signs, parables, analogies, and the like — rhetorical forms that are at once vivid and interpretationally fixed, inasmuch as they contain a limited and discoverable number of possible meanings. "Beware of false prophets, which come to you in sheep's clothing, but inwardly they are ravening wolves," Jesus says in Matthew 7:15, and we know just what the sheep's clothing is, what the wolves are. We're supposed to, because the early Christians, like Jesus himself, for the most part wanted to be clear, to instruct and to convince. It is a proselytizing religion: the message is meant to be understood by as many people as possible. And while I don't mean to suggest that the whole of the New Testament is perfectly transparent — of course there are some mysteries, the Trinity being an obvious example, that are to be contemplated under the aegis of faith rather than understanding — there does seem to be some sense in which the forms of evangelical language are bounded by the desire to save the souls of ordinary men.

Moreover, and more interestingly, Christian poetics manifests the religion it describes. Because to represent things as the New Testament does is to suggest that the world is a kind of puzzle to be deciphered, a rebus with an answer: the way and the truth are hidden, but not so deeply that they can't be unveiled. To reveal them is to reveal their sense, to uncover the moral logic that lies beneath the world we experience. The lesson is love, the result is saintliness, and the final reward is salvation.

By contrast, Jewish sacred writing, particularly in the Torah, seems to me to be emphatically literal. Metaphors do sometimes occur, but they're secondary and ornamental; anyway, deciphering them isn't going to lead to greater understanding of the faith. The real force of Hebrew poetics comes not from its figuration, but from its leaping juxtapositions and buried motivations; the art succeeds by forswearing artifice, by begging any interpretation and demanding instead to be pondered as it is, an inscrutable, exigent, fearsome thing.

Consider Moses, for example, innocently tending his father-in-law's flock in chapter 3 of Exodus when he receives a sudden visitation: "And the angel of the LORD appeared unto him in a flame of fire out of the midst of a bush: and he looked, and, behold, the bush burned with fire, and the bush was not consumed." It's a startling transition, and the result is a kind of poetry, but there is, the zealously exegetical rabbinical tradition notwithstanding, no sense in asking what it means. It *means* just what it *says,* that is, that the angel of the Lord appeared unto him in a flame of fire, etc. "I AM THAT I AM," Yahweh says to Moses out of that burning bush, and one dare not ask any further. The same might be said of his book: its stories and pronouncements are not images, or metaphors, or parables, or symbols; indeed they exist, in their singular and irreducible being, precisely to be none of those things. What you see is what you get, and what you get is mystery enough. And that, I would argue, suggests a conception of God such that he's to be feared and obeyed: the lesson is piety, the result is righteousness, and the final reward is the Promised Land.

Style *is* religion. How a piece of writing renders the world shows how its author sees the world, sees cosmology, causality, virtue, evil, beauty, and so on. Such things reside in connectives and articles, in punctuation, in the interstices between images, in the lapses between a noun and its verb — down in the gutters of prose. That insight may be the oldest in all of literature, but it's one that each writer discovers for him- or herself. I learned it in large part by contemplating the differences between the Jewish and Christian Bibles.

I want, therefore, to take a piece of the New Testament that I particularly admire and show how Christian figuration works, roughly following what I gather is a standard reading. At the same time, I want to show how it gets its power by drawing upon the power of the very Judaism that it would render otiose. What interests me, then, is both how the New Testament creates Christianity and how the Old Testament became the *Old* Testament, rather than simply the Testament.

As exemplar, I'll use the opening proem of the Gospel According to John, because it seems to me to be a passage of extraordinary ambition, power, and compression, qualities manifest in its very first line. "In the beginning was the Word," says John, "and the Word was with God, and the Word was God." And immediately one recognizes the voice of an author who sets no bounds on the history that is his to take.

Indeed, as an opener this is not just lapidary, but nearly hubristic. With his very first words, John announces his intention to compete with Genesis itself, to begin where it begins, at the very opening threshold of time. Compare this with the modesty of the other Gospels: Matthew starts with his feet firmly planted in earthly history, in the generations of man leading up to the birth of Jesus. Mark merely announces that his book brings good news, and begins his narrative with the efforts of John the Baptist. Luke, always the most down-to-earth of the four, begins his story with a bit of throat-clearing salutation before launching into an even more recent history, that is, an account of the events immediately preceding the births of both John the Baptist and Jesus.

Each of the four wants to legitimate the story of Jesus by situating it within the history of Judaism, and each has a different way of doing so. Mark is the most perfunctory, merely citing the prophecy of a coming Messiah, using what, so far as I can tell, is a passage from the relatively obscure Book of Malachi. But Matthew and Luke are more canny: both seem to recognize that the narrative of the Hebrew Bible is structured around birth and blood, that the political history of the Jews is tantamount to the family history of the descendants of Noah.

After all, God's most common injunction to the Jews in Genesis is to be fruitful, and multiply, and the drama of the book grows out of their attempts to keep it, through floods and familial strife, bouts of incest and betrayal, and, perhaps most ironically of all, through the barrenness of the three aged matriarchs. Such crises of generation are the cliff-hangers of Jewish history; the tension and release of Genesis's plot occur as each obstacle is met and somehow overcome, and the result is a religious narrative that blurs the distinction between the Jews as a race and Judaism as a religion.

That's why Matthew begins by calling his Gospel "The book of the generation of Jesus Christ, the son of David, the son of Abraham." Such a genealogy is meant to prove Jesus' blood link to the Jewish past, to establish him as the heir to Jewish history, hence to place the Christianity he inspires on a continuum with its Hebrew counterpart. For to do so is to sanction the new religion under the terms of the old one, and to pave the way for the idea that Christ represents not just another step in Jewish history, but the last step: Judaism's completion, its fulfillment and the cause of its obsolescence.

Luke, too, draws upon Genesis, but in a more subtle way. Rather than simply proposing Jesus as the latest blossom on the Jewish family tree, he rather cleverly mimics the plot devices he finds in the midsection of Genesis. For Luke has the mind of a novelist, and what he borrows to accredit his own prophet is not historical content but narrative form. So he makes his Elisabeth barren just as Sarah is in Genesis 17, Rebecca is in Genesis 25, and Rachel is in Genesis 29, and we are meant to conclude that her son, John the Baptist, is blessed just as Isaac, Jacob, and Joseph were; and Mary's virginity is its own kind of crisis, perhaps the ultimate kind, and it comes with an even more spectacular solution.

But John's assimilation of Judaism into Christianity reaches further than any of these. For there are three kinds of history at stake in the New Testament: divine, political, and personal: that is, the history of heaven, the history of man, and the history of Jesus. The authors of the Gospels are obligated to tell all three, to wind them together into one narrative, but only John has the confidence to assume that divine history is the background against which the other two occur, rather than being a mystic realm that intersects with human history only in brief and separated moments of godly meddling, and to assume, too, that he has a poetic right to tell it that way.

"In the beginning" — again — "was the Word, and the Word was with God, and the Word was God." My concern here, then, is less with the various meanings of "Word" and more with the meanings of "was," for John uses that verb some ten times in the first eighty-three words of his Gospel, and it's in his enormously subtle, complex, and supple sense of time and tense that he first proves his genius. There are three occurrences of "was" in the first line alone, each of them distinct in meaning, intention, and result. The first is a temporal mark, delineating the rearmost border of time itself, the sense in which the Word existed as soon as anything existed, and has always been waiting for us; the Word frames time itself; it's the background against which all other history occurs. The second "was" is predicative, identifying the Word as a property of God, or if not a property, then perhaps a possession, or a feature, or a trait — whatever relation we might posit between a person's voice and the person. The third "was" is that of simple identity, used here to assert that God is the Word, and the Word is God. It is a description that is, logically speaking, incompatible with the previous one, but that, I assume, is just the point: it's as if John wants to surround God's Word itself, entangling it in a net of verbs as a way of pinning down its incomprehensible status in time.

After such an extraordinary burst of poetry, John takes a bit of a breather; the next verse simply reiterates the first, and the third directs us to a relatively straightforward function of God, that is, as the creator of everything that exists. Temporally, however, 1:3 is crucial, because it's here that John begins to move his poem out of its initial timeless stasis and into a world in which events occur; for while the making of things to which he refers is left otherwise undescribed, we know that John's pattern here is to mimic the start of Genesis, and we know that God's creation in that book happens day by day. We have breached the membrane that separates the motionless eternal from earthly time and have begun to move forward toward the start of human history.

The shifting quickens in 1:4, and the web of metaphors that allows John to surround Judaism begins to take shape, but we can be excused for not recognizing it right away, given that we've become conditioned to tracking John's Gospel against Genesis.

"In him," he says, "was life; and the life was the light of men," and we remember that God's first utterance is "Light!" It is, strictly speaking, his first Word, his first emanation, so we might be tempted to conclude that John has simply embellished the symbolism of Creation by proposing the Word, life, and the light as three facets of a single divine presence. But, as I suggested above, this kind of extended figurative equation is relatively unknown in early Hebrew writing, and the alert reader might notice that John has begun to change the rhetorical basis of his book, turning it into something new and foreign to its ostensible source.

Indeed, with the very next line — "And the light shineth in darkness; and the darkness comprehended it not" — John's telling of Creation takes on an unexpected spin as he begins to guide his readers toward the interpretation he's proposing. The failure of the darkness to acknowledge or understand the light that has burst forth within it suggests a conflict unlike anything we find in those first verses of Genesis, which, until now, have served as John's model. Still, it's unclear at this stage whether this is mere personification or some deeper metaphoric effort, whether, that is, the action is complete as it's described or a quick foreshadowing that sets up the plot to follow. And so we wait to see.

We'll have to wait a little while, because here John does something brilliant and unexpected; the story takes an abrupt and startling turn. After moving from abstraction and eternity into a moment of anticipatory tension, John defers his drama. Instead, an individual man, real and historically situated, is suddenly dropped into the story, like the crystal that seeds a solution. "There was a man sent from God, whose name was John": in eleven words John shifts his narrative from divine time, divine history, divine being, to something more human and immediate, and does so by using the same verb — "There *was* a man" — but twisting it to tell of a sublunar being.

There's reason, I know, to believe that this development isn't John's work at all, but the result of a later redactor somewhat crudely stitching together two entirely different texts. But by my understanding of John as a writer, it's perfectly plausible that he should have been the sole engineer of these lines. I've already suggested that this sort of sudden shift is common in the Hebrew Bible, for that book is willfully strange when it comes to narrative. Major changes — a visit from God, a new story line, a revelation — are generally announced with no preparation beyond the word "And . . . ," or at best, "And then . . ." Genealogical tables, inscrutable remarks, brutally abrupt resolutions, appear without introduction or explanation. In fact, such unexpected turns and cuts are the very basis of Hebrew poetics: the Jewish God is nothing if not unpredictable, a ceaseless and often frightening surprise, and his habitual suspension of the laws of causality and reason is mirrored in the narrative flow of his book. With that in mind, the transition from John 1:5 to 1:6 seems less like an editorial accident and more like a deliberate act of homage, and it enforces my belief that John is the Gospel author most aware of the subtleties of his Jewish precedents, not just as political history, but as divine inspiration and poetic achievement.

What's more, it soon becomes clear that he wants to complete the metaphor that he began in 1:4–5, even if he insists on doing so slowly, by backing into it. In the lines following, John the Baptist is described, somewhat dismissively, as being not the Light itself, but the witness to the Light; Jesus is not directly introduced, still less identified as the Light. Instead we meet him in roundabout fashion, through the medium of John the Baptist as witness, and the delay produces a tension that is not resolved until 1:10, where we learn that the Light is a man, a messiah, and so too is the Word, and the life, all four elements being identical and creating, with their combined weight, a single, overarching Good. It is a remarkable tactic, the more so in that it ends as it begins, with the word "was" — "He *was* in the world" — used this time to locate the divine Jesus in the earthly world.

As far as my own reading goes, the main work of John's proem is about finished there. In ten verses of extraordinary subtlety and compression, he's recast the history of the world in such a way as to make the appearance of the Christ seem not just believable, but inevitable. The rest of the chapter serves to cash out the consequences of the symbolic pattern that he has so ingeniously established, and the writing shifts from history to doctrine, which means much less to me. But I do want to point to two later verses that I find striking, both of them again pivoting around the word "was."

The first is John the Baptist's cry in 1:15: "He that cometh after me is preferred before me: for he was before me." That's a paradox, of course, but it's not just John the Baptist's; it's precisely the paradox that John proposes to the Jews. The other three Gospels argue that Christianity is the next step in Jewish history. John's argument, presented through metaphor and completed almost before one notices it, is even deeper: Judaism, he claims, was always Christianity, because Christianity was as soon as Judaism was, and perhaps just a moment sooner. For Christ is the Word of Creation, he is God's original emanation, and while he comes after, he nevertheless always existed before.

The second line that stands out from the remainder of John's proem occurs two verses later, when Judaism is dismissed almost in passing: "For the law was given by Moses, but grace and truth came from Jesus Christ." It is intended as a death knell, that particular "was"; it resounds with a pastness that no previous occurrence of the word quite attained, as if it meant, "was, but very definitely is no longer." The evangelists as a group were, of course, somewhat ambiguous about the status of Jewish law after the death of the Messiah; we know, from this "was," where John stands on the matter. It's the last occasion upon which the word appears in the proem, and it has, to these ears at least, a dark and minatory ring.

Because whatever the merits of the other books of the New Testament may be, as moral law, poetics, or history, they simply aren't mine. I couldn't imagine believing in the world as they describe it. So they exist for me as a sort of anthropological curiosity, a guide to the thinking of the people who surround me, and I read them with a fair amount of detachment. By my lights, Revelation is an impressive and entertaining eschatological rant, Luke's Gospel a touching, patient explanation, and Paul — well, I've got to admit that I find Paul contemptible, for more reasons than I can go into here. But John . . .

He would have made a good Jew — a weird and somewhat presumptuous compliment to offer in this context, I know, the more so inasmuch as John is the most eager of the evangelists to blame the Jews for the death of Christ. He may indeed have been the only real anti-Semite among them; I'll leave it to those more practiced in literary psychoanalysis to suggest whence his hatred springs. I can nevertheless concede that he wrote an astonishing piece of poetry, and I admit to a certain admiration for his argument, even if his conclusion is that my own people are just a placeholder in God's grand design. I don't believe him for a moment, of course, and I don't like him, but I can appreciate him.

Because of all the Gospel authors, John seems to me to have the fullest appreciation of what history is and how it can be transformed, of what poetry is and how it can be used, of what language is and how history and poetry reside in its depths. Writing in another context, I once suggested that Christianity was an improbable thing, given the political realities of the world in which it arose; I suspect that writing like John's proem was all that kept it from being impossible.

Teenage Jesus

Ann Powers

LIKE most hamburger-nourished, television-tutored American millennial kids, I spent a serious chunk of my youth arguing with my father at the dinner table. I don't remember much from these exchanges, only the mood — tense veering into hysterical — and the image of Dad, still in his navy blue workday suit, trying to concentrate on his pork chop while this small chubby demon in a "Question Authority" T-shirt shouted at him from behind her Jell-O plate. I also remember the subject of many of the fights. My father and I, in some primitive way, were debating the nature of God.

My father possesses a deep, anti-articulate belief in Christianity. Raised Irish Catholic by a mother who loved to have priests over for tea, he probably would never have rebelled against his upbringing; at any rate, his fate was sealed at nineteen. Mortally wounded in the French field during World War II, he made a deal with his Maker, and, surviving, he kept his word: in matters of the spirit, Dad does not ask questions. I, on the other hand, was born to be contrary and curious about the shape, taste, smell, and purpose of the Divine. If, as Augustine suggests, the restless search for God is an adolescent one, then I am forever seventeen.

Imagine my delight when I discovered that Jesus was a brat who fought with his parents, too. The story's in Luke, at the climax of that Gospel's unusually long infancy narrative. The family visits Jerusalem at Passover; at twelve, Jesus is just embarking on a year of fasting and preparation for his bar mitzvah. After the holiday ends, Mary and Joseph head back toward Galilee. Assuming their son's hanging out with his cousins at the other end of the caravan, they don't notice he's played hooky until they're a day away from the temple. Frantic, they return and scour Jerusalem for him. If milk cartons had existed in those days, Jesus' mug would have been on one.

After three days, they find him where they should have looked in the first place. Why do parents so rarely bother to learn the details of their kids' preoccupations? You look for a beach bum at the surf shop, for a rocker at the record store. Jesus, philosophy head that he was, stayed behind at the temple to catch a buzz from the wise guys there. As the passage reads, he's deep into a conversation with them when his parents barge in. Mary scolds Jesus in front of his new friends. How embarrassing. Jesus answers with stinging, sullen disdain. " 'Why were you looking for me?' he replied. 'Did you not know that I would be in my Father's house?' " Mary, for once living up to the limits of her parental role, doesn't understand.

Some versions of Luke cite Jesus' response as "I must be busy with my Father's affairs," but I prefer to think that Jesus went right for his folks' jugular, snidely suggesting that he shouldn't even be living with them. His query echoes the most basic question of the insecure youth: *How could these alien creatures possibly be my parents?* Of course, the twist with Jesus is that he really has landed in the wrong family. We all know who his real father is, and now that Yahweh's seen his kid in his own house — witnessed how well Jesus fits in here, how natural it feels — he's demanding joint custody.

Traditional readings of this passage minimize the conflict between Jesus and his human family. Joseph and Mary aren't amazed by Jesus' nerve, these interpretations say, but by his emergent spiritual power; their shock recalls the disbelief of wonder-kid elders from King David's clan to Clark Kent's ma and pa. Miracle tales from the twelfth year of a hero's life are common: Moses, Samuel, Epicurus, and Josephus all had experiences predicting their vocations at that age. And teen rebellion didn't really factor into the private life of the ancient world, since the concept of adolescence hadn't developed yet. Most Gospel readers view this incident as nothing other than a lively sign of Jesus' true identity and later mission.

Yet, as A. N. Wilson has noted, the Jesus of the Gospels often displayed a disdain for earthly family ties that went beyond mere identification with his divine deadbeat dad. His rebuke of Mary in the temple is just the start of a lifetime of being mean to Mom, and of renouncing family values in general. At the wedding in Cana, recorded in John's Gospel, Jesus snaps at Mary when she asks him to turn water into wine, although he then dutifully delivers the miracle. Throughout his apostasy, he exhorts his followers to cast off their kin, even dismissing one disciple's desire to give his father a funeral with the flip rejoinder "Let the dead bury the dead." And he rejects his mother once again when she and his brothers, worried he might be losing his marbles, seek him out at Capernaum: "Who are my mother and my brothers?" he says. The answer comes quickly: anybody who does the will of God — anybody, it seems, but Jesus' actual relatives.

Jesus himself enjoyed a prolonged, if not perpetual, adolescence.

Jesus never set down roots, didn't work a straight job, ran with a wild crowd, partied a lot, and avoided wearing shoes. Like a rock star, he had an entourage of fast women who cared for his needs and a posse of guys who hung on his every word. His mother was not the only person he showered with disrespect — he behaved with equal impropriety toward priests and cops. Jesus spoke his mind and followed his bliss. There's a lot for a kid to admire in that.

I envision the boy Christ in the temple as the adolescent spirit personified: his face turning nine shades of red, his voice tight with frustration at his parents' utter cluelessness. The answers he offers Mary hardly resonate with spiritual wisdom; they're curt and mean, and then he gives her the silent treatment. Whatever the passage's prophetic purpose for Luke, as a story it makes sense to the bored and fidgety teen who hears it read at Sunday Mass, who also wants to start his life *right now,* choose his own friends, and keep some of his secrets to himself. Jesus would maintain his bratty edge throughout his life. But brattiness does not inhabit the core of adolescence; it's an outgrowth, like pimples. On a deeper level, the skepticism of youth signals the beginning of a search for something actually worth trusting, both within one's own psyche and in the world. That's why teens, supposedly stuck in life's lost years, are often so unequivocal about what they love and what they hate, and so frustrated when they feel misunderstood. The adolescent spirit is not the spirit of the lost. It is the conviction that you are not lost — that wandering has a purpose, and that what you deserve more than anything is the freedom to walk a while on your own path.

CHRISTIANS caught on to the possibilities of the teen-Jesus connection in the waning days of the 1960s cultural revolution. The hippie dream of LSD and tantric revelation began to crash, as did its complement, the grassroots embrace of revolutionary politics; many burned-out seekers wished for a simpler, safer way to turn on and drop out. Jesus provided one answer. Jesus freaks (or, as they preferred to be called, Jesus People) became a phenomenon in 1971, with *Look, Life, Time,* NBC, and CBS simultaneously trumpeting their takeover of the youth movement. Teens and twentysomethings all over the country joined communes and youth groups that practiced fundamentalist Christianity in the guise of radical proletarianism. Their conversions came upon them like bouts of Beatlemania, their connection to a hippiefied Christ as intense and unquestioning as puppy love. Their Jesus may have looked like a long-haired John Lennon, but for these kids, he functioned more like a forgiving dad. *Time* reported that one freak suddenly converted in the midst of a depression caused by the deaths of Martin Luther King Jr. and Robert F. Kennedy. "It was the last thing I expected," she said of her newfound zeal.

The Jesus-freak scene centered on the quick-fix capital, Los Angeles. Its leaders discouraged leftist politics and cultivated a narcissistic, passive attitude in their acolytes. Theology remained scarce among Jesus People, while displays of childlike trust abounded. Their naïveté recalls the other flocks that formed as the counterculture's spirit grew decadent: followers of various Eastern gurus, the Symbionese Liberation Army, even the cult of Jim Jones. Although less menacing, the cult of the Jesus freaks ultimately proved as manipulative. What seemed on the surface to be a radicalization of Christianity itself proved to be just another way of dressing up glassy-eyed fundamentalism.

Jesus freakdom quickly faded, but the excitement it generated impressed the priests and ministers in charge of many traditional Christian institutions. The Jesus People proved that aspects of the counterculture, and of youth culture in general, could be adapted to serve Christianity. Ministers from Billy Graham on down penned tracts extolling the vision of these burlap-wearing weirdos, recognizing how normal they were deep down inside. What they didn't see as easily was that a real youth-centered Christianity would change the focus of the church, if not on a grand scale, then in the way it worked in many people's lives.

For Catholics, in the rush of change following Vatican II, Jesus as hippie became the center of a new way to sell Christ to kids. Folk masses allowed young people to sing praise to the tune of soft-rock radio (I remember my folk group being particularly proud of an arrangement of Elton John's "Love Is the Opening Door," suitable for postcommunion meditation). *Good News for Modern Man* and *The Way* brought the Gospels into paperback, complete with funky covers and occasional slang. Parochial school curricula replaced the Baltimore Catechism with Salinger's *Franny and Zooey* and the poems of e. e. cummings. The songs from *Godspell* became the sound track to our school masses and graduations. It became possible to believe in a totally teenage church.

The prime example of the church's seismic shift regarding youth culture was the about-face concerning *Jesus Christ Superstar.* "I wouldn't walk across the street to see that film!" my mother exclaimed when it opened at our neighborhood theater in 1973. The Council of Bishops had declared director Norman Jewison's version of the Andrew Lloyd Webber–Tim Rice rock opera blasphemous for its implications about Jesus' sex life (vague) and lack of resurrection (even vaguer, as I later found out). By the time I hit senior year in 1981, though, the bishops had reconsidered, and *JCS* was a welcome element of our religious instruction. As our "Christian Themes in Literature" teacher, Mrs. Ketter, explained, somebody had discovered the extremely faint presence of a shepherd leading his flock past the empty cross in the closing frames of the film, not to mention the candlelight in the last frame. The shepherd's a shadow, the light's a blip — no matter, said Mrs. Ketter. Their presence meant Mr. Jewison did believe in the risen Christ. As for Mary Magdalene, well, that was just infatuation.

Watching *JCS* again, I can see why Mrs. Ketter and her peers wanted us seventeen-year-olds to see it. The film so wrenchingly portrays adolescent desire that it's still painful for me to watch, long after I put my own high school obsessions (the worst focused on Paul McCartney and student council president John Mc-Clure) to rest. Anguished close-ups of Yvonne Elliman as Mary Magdelene and Carl Anderson as Judas reveal their motivation: they'll do anything, whether it means betraying their Lord or enduring the sight of his death, to get him to notice them. "Why don't you listen to me?" screeches Anderson in the first scene, sealing his fate as the bad kid who acts out to get attention. Elliman is gentler, more wishful than angry. "Could we start again, please?" she quietly begs as Ted Neeley's Jesus walks away for the last time. Neeley forever walks away from his loved ones; he's doomed by his destiny to disappoint. The most sacreligious element in this film is not its treatment of Christ as a mortal man, but its suggestion that Jesus, given to a higher purpose, can't satisfy anyone's personal desire.

Neeley's faraway eyes reveal the reason Jesus keeps walking: he wants to try to catch up with some answers of his own. The Gethsemane scene gets a heavy-metal treatment in *JCS;* veins bulging, Neeley yowls out Christ's famous "Why must I die?" as a venomous rebel cry; he accepts his fate frustratedly, his question unanswered. His adolescent spirit refuses to simply accept; he wants justification. This demand goes for parents, teachers, the law, and God, too. "Faith cannot be shaken," writes the philosopher Jacob Needleman. "It is the result of being shaken." The adolescent shakes and shakes until what she needs falls into place. At Gethsemane, Jesus asked a question, and as a boy Jesus came to the temple to ask questions; although he carries the certainty of self within, he begins and ends his ministry as a searcher. Shake me, he says.

At the same time, the adolescent spirit seeks a place to rest. Despite what their elders think, kids rarely cause disruption for its own sake. They want genuine safety, for their souls as well as their bodies, and they'll rattle the cage to stop it from damaging them or to get someone to notice their need. Christian institutions have worked hard since the 1960s to establish ways this disruption can be both cultivated and contained. The thriving Christian rock industry provides the best example. "Why should a religion of mystery and beauty produce music so cheesy, so obvious?" asks rock critic Will Hermes in a 1996 essay from *Request* magazine. Later he explains: "Ambiguity and doubt get passed over in favor of reaffirming pabulum, and like all commercial pop, an aesthetic pack mentality overrides that of the unique individual." Hermes is right about the bathetic quality of most official God-rock; it's awful. But why, then, does it continue to burgeon in popularity? L. A. Kauffman, writing about an antisex fundamentalist concert for the *Nation,* hits on the reason when she notes that despite the event's puritan message, the music itself "throbbed with erotic energy," got the kids screaming, drove them a little wild. Even the tamest, lamest rock can have this effect, which comes from the music's rhythmic root. By tapping into rock's basic restlessness as a counterpoint to their repressive messages, fundamentalists have found a way to viscerally persuade kids of the freedom in containment. Such methods fool the adolescent spirit into believing it's being honored when it's being squashed.

Today, Christian elders know that kids need to search for themselves, but remain fearful of what those kids might find. Since the 1960s, when the dialogue began in earnest, young Christians have continued to complain about being babied, controlled, condescended to. Much experimentation has occurred within high schools, Sunday and summer programs, and congregational groups since then, but too often, the simplistic messages offered teens ("sex is bad," for example) fail them as they continue to grow. The rush of being born again can stimulate youthful loyalty to a church, but this kind of devotion rarely lasts. If it's going to last, the spiritual encounter can't just be a crush. Even a teenager knows that.

When I was a baby bohemian trying to find my place in the spirit's house, my relationship to Catholicism was, to put it mildly, schizophrenic. I could easily go from a wholesome morning singing "Day by Day" in the school choir to a heathen night of LSD and making out with my college-age boyfriend. Both ways of spending my time gave me pleasure and taught me something. Did I see a contradiction here? Not in the least. Was there one to see? Even now, having fought for years to reconcile with a religion that condemns my gay loved ones and considers me unequal because I am a woman, I don't think so. Doctrine is one thing, mystical experience another. Sacredness spills over in sex and psychedelics, and in prayer, ritual, song. Before I became adult, resigned to other people's judgments, I refused to distinguish one leap into possibility from another.

Adolescents are often accused of narcissism, and their cruel insensitivity to others is legendary. But a side of that self-absorption feeds the spiritual search in ways that we forget as we grow older. Habit-bound, we often stop noticing ourselves. We no longer move as we did, in many directions, just to see how each new one would feel, and more importantly, to see how we do in each new situation, what it might make of us, whether we can master it. The teenage dare can be reckless and stupid. At its heart, though, is the important need for a system of belief not motivated by outside sources, but by the higher authority of the self. On its downside, such a fight for independence results in shallow selfishness. At its best, it creates the only authority that lasts.

I continue to try to honor this spirit within myself. But I'm more than ten years out of my teens, and despite the fact that I sometimes still get carded at the liquor store, I don't really know what it's like to be an adolescent now. I wondered whether I was romanticizing a period in my life that in many ways was messy and painful. So I did a little fieldwork. Sister Judy Frasinetti of the Greater New York Catholic Youth Organization (CYO) guided me to Blair Lodge, a weekend retreat house neer Peekskill, where Catholic teens gather to explore their faith and cement their commitment to God.

My high school participated in a program similar to the one I'd be witnessing. It was called Search, and I never went on one, although my best friend did, our junior year. She returned from the weekend with spooky eyes and an orange ribbon she wrapped around my wrist; "I can't tell you what we did there," she whispered, "but this ribbon means you're the right kind of person to go on one, too." *Eww,* I thought as I gave her a wan smile and departed for my philosophy class. I'd heard about Charles Manson and the Moonies; I even knew someone whose brother lived under the ground in Montana with the Elizabeth Clare Prophet people. I didn't care if Search was Catholic. No cults for me.

Now I realize that I simply didn't need Search the way my

friend apparently did. Rock and roll had already found me; I had my imaginary community and my real friends who believed in the same higher power — the Clash — that I did. The cesspool of high school social life, with its judgmental rules about identity ("He's so fat!") and behavior ("She lets him/She doesn't let him!") swirled over my feet, but I'd found a little ledge to perch on. The kids I met at Blair Lodge had no other ledge — not because their lives were so desperate, although some were, and not because they were social outcasts, because none seemed to be. These were average kids who hadn't found any other shelter where they could rest within their restlessness, admitting to their confusion, their fears, their vulnerability, and also their authority, their strengths. And so they came to this Christian place, not so much to explore religion as to look into each other's, and their own, mixed-up hearts.

This was not what I expected from Blair Lodge. I thought I'd find a bunch of pious little pricks in pro-life T-shirts making antigay jokes. I did spy one such T-shirt (on a counselor) and heard one such joke (from a different counselor), but the kids themselves displayed a remarkable tolerance and curiosity. "I ask my father millions of questions about everything," said one girl. "Questions that don't even make sense." At lunch, a boy admitted that he occasionally drank and even had sex, but he'd given up both vices for Lent. "Is oral sex wrong?" he asked the room. A dozen groans and "Yes, you idiot"s answered him, but the air remained free of criticism. This was just Delmore, the group's wild child, still learning. Later in the afternoon, the girl with the million questions (call her Cathy) spoke of a friend who was considering an abortion. She knew what she believed about the practice, she said, but she planned to stand by her friend. "She believes in God, but she's young. It's her life."

Although they studiously avoided judging the outside world, these kids clearly wanted some help surviving in it. They used Christianity like a rope thrown down from the top of a cliff they were trying to climb. CYO gave them a way to say no to drugs and to drinking without looking foolish; it replaced the schoolground pressure cooker with a scene centered around Christian-flavored learning, sharing, and introspection. During the session known as "Question Box," when head counselor Luis answered "your hardest questions," the kids challenged him on subjects ranging from the existence of limbo to the rights of homosexuals and the verity of the Adam and Eve myth. His answers definitely steered the kids toward accepting Catholic dictums, but he always phrased them in terms of choice, not judgment. "If you want to be in this religion, you have to play by its rules" was his good-cop message. Taking this in, the kids behaved like students, but ones without fear of being laughed at; they admitted their pain and even their ignorance unhesitatingly. Even more impressive, in casual moments they treated each other with an affection and openness I had never seen before. No uptight Christians here: boys and girls and girls and boys hugged each other, danced together in spontaneous outbursts, and yelled their anger or their joy at the top of their lungs. It was understood that they'd make mistakes and that each would run away from time to time. They were trying to give each other a light to carry out there.

"Since I've been in CYO I see myself as a different person and I really like the person I see," said a girl I'll call Janet. Before, Janet was the kind of person who didn't talk to friends, let alone strangers. "Put me in a corner all night and I was happy," she said. But then she came to a Blair weekend a year ago and met Susie, and Susie brought her out of her shell. "Now you can't shut me up!" But it wasn't just her newfound pal who changed Janet's life; it was the fact that beyond that one friendship, she was embraced. "Last night during prayer service I went to light a candle, and I just couldn't do it," she admitted. "I was crying too hard, and I just sat down, and five people came over to me and put their arms around me."

These kids were in many ways still sheep outside the fold, and not one showed any superiority to another. Some had lost parents, siblings, or boyfriends to death; others had traumatic home lives. All were enduring the anxieties of trying to transform from child to adult. "If I have a problem, I know that I can call someone from CYO, because chances are they've already had that problem," said Susie. These young people had seen each other at their worst and not walked away. That's not something every high schooler can say of his supposed best friends.

The limits of this intense communal spirit won't be tested until the CYO kids make their way out into the world. They rely heavily on each other, and that could become a problem; many kids admit that their non-CYO relationships have suffered since they joined. The warm bubble of Blair could become a trap for some. Although the group I met was extremely diverse racially, classwise, and even in terms of rural or urban upbringing, each teen stressed their similarities and didn't show that much awareness of their differences. Yet even if the group does drift apart, I couldn't help thinking how lucky these kids were to have built this shelter for a while.

And what did Jesus have to do with Blair Lodge? I asked Ted, one of the peer counselors, that question as he drove me back to the train station. "So much is changing during this part of our lives," he said. "We'll all be there for each other, but if no one else is there, you can always talk to Jesus. And he'll listen and be there for you." This image of Jesus as the ultimate imaginary friend seemed very much intended for the child side of the Blair Lodge kids — a bit soft. But I noticed that Ted didn't say Jesus would solve the predicaments he was facing in his first year of college, and I remembered Cathy, talking earlier in the day, describing the anger and confusion she'd felt when her boyfriend had died in a car crash the year before. "I feel like he's in heaven," she'd said. Then a double take. "Not like he was a perfect boy." CYO had given her a place to work out her confusion about the need to be perfect and the right to wonder why. For her and the other Blair Lodge kids, Jesus isn't as much a savior as a sounding board, a therapist, maybe, a parent who'll never feel disappointed in you. A pal, most of all. This Jesus only has one desire: to let you be yourself.

The adolescent spirit is the part of us that goes wandering but always returns home. During our teen years, we feel trapped within our weaknesses and defensive about our strengths; as we mature, that "restless weariness," as Augustine calls it, becomes the itch to forever test the parameters of possibility, of love. The Jesus we meet in the Gospels is full of this impulse to argue and to seek, and any Christian practice must make room for it. I think of the prodigal son, another story only found in Luke and probably the favorite Gospel passage among the teens I've known. After his time on the road, the son can offer the father he rejected nothing. He still does not look or act like an adult. But he has learned something, that is clear. "It is only right we should celebrate," says that father, sick of arguing. And the son realizes that the whole point of getting lost was to have the chance to find his own way back.

My God

Lucy Grealy

My God, My God, why hast Thou forsaken me?
MARK 15:34 / MATTHEW 27:46

Father, forgive them: they know not what they do.
LUKE 23:34

It is finished.
JOHN 19:30

M Y early religious education, to the age of six, consisted of memorizing all the words to the rock opera *Jesus Christ Superstar.* Actually, I did more than memorize them, I acted out the whole album, my own private version of the London musical, which opened earlier than the American. I combined my passion for this album with my crush on Mr. Ed, the talking horse. I had one of those innocent crushes that couldn't distinguish between loving Mr. Ed and wanting to *be* Mr. Ed, and I'd re-create the entire drama of Jesus and Judas and the other apostles as a talking horse. All this took place on a large yellow Chinese carpet that lay in front of the stereo in the living room. Each part of the carpet signified a character, and I would canter on my hands and knees from corner to corner to mouth each part as it came up. My knees carpet-burning into a vivid red, I performed the entire drama single-handedly.

For the big chorus parts, I would mount my Hippity-Hop, a sort of big red rubber ball on which you could sit and propel yourself by holding onto a half-circle handle and bouncing. I'd race around the room, imagining that I was riding in complicated formation, banners flapping, as the apostles wondered what was happening, as the beggars and lepers overtook Jesus, as the crowd jeered, in harmony, for his crucifixion. The only drawback to the choruses was that my bouncing about often made the needle skip on the record, but it was also necessary, as it gave my knees a short rest. It wasn't the performance that made me love the album; that had to do with my courtship of the strong, safe, gleamingly visceral world of Mr. Ed. The music itself had an uncanny hold on me; the sways and turns of the emotional narrative entranced me, even, and maybe especially, when I didn't understand them. The Pharisees were my favorites because their voices were so exotically varied, plus they all seemed so confused and put-upon, which, even at six, was a state I identified with. I had to hold my ears during the scene in which Jesus was whipped by the forty-nine lashes, not because I felt bad for him, but because the music itself seemed so dreadful.

NOT surprisingly, for the rest of my childhood I held a rather liberal take on the New Testament. Jesus obviously possessed quite a number of very human failings, and though I knew from other sources, such as early morning Sunday television, that he was a very kind person, he seemed fairly preoccupied a lot of the time in the gospel according to Andrew Lloyd Webber. I liked Judas far better and felt very sorry when he killed himself: in truth, he seemed like the only one with any deep feelings at all, and I thought he'd been unjustly set up. He also had a much better singing voice. This was all I knew, and even this I kept to myself. Religion, in my family, was regarded as a highly specialized form of stupidity.

A few years later, when I was about ten and very ill, I began receiving letters of "hope and encouragement" from people I'd never met before, strangers who'd heard about a disfiguring affliction I had and wrote in the hope of cheering me up. Each and every one of these letters eventually got around to God. Had I accepted him as my savior? How could these poor people ever guess the ridicule their letters received? My cynical older brothers, whose nasty humor I confused with worldliness, loved to read the letters out loud in the kitchen. Most of the letters were written in a rounded, overly even hand that I learned to recognize when I began teaching more than a decade later as the generic handwriting of a dull education. My brothers, nine and thirteen years older than I, had been educated in Ireland, and their teachers had all been priests. I don't think I had ever actually met a priest, not face-to-face. These letters caused my brothers to thicken and coarsen their accents, imitating specific priests they'd both known. "Have you accepted Jesus Christ as your savior, young girl?" they'd ask me in their strange voices, adding odd and specific physical tics — eyes that roamed leftward, hands that trembled — that pushed them over the edge into tearful hysteria. Left out of the joke, I could only pause and feel jealous, learning by osmosis that anyone who believed such things as these letters hinted at was a certifiable fool.

Still, there was a part of me that longed to believe. If I believed, then perhaps I would be happy. My life at the time, due to my illness and the insanity endemic to my family, was outlined with every conceivable type of emotional, physical, social, and psychic pain. Luckily, my interior life was up for the job, and the world I inhabited, though by this time less outwardly silly than pretending I was a talking horse playing out the New Testament, coursed like a fast stream over solidly built fantasies. I barely knew who I was, only who I pretended to be: a pony express rider, a space alien, an unrecognized genius, all of us flailing around in the white water of a desperate escape.

Some of the letters also contained pamphlets. I would sit at the kitchen table, the cats rubbing around my legs, and read stories of saintly people who were able to bear any hardship, whether it was illness, solitude, poverty, or the scorn of others, with a grace that actually shone from them in the illustrations — shards of light emanating from the believer's head, depending upon the illustrator's skill, like either soft mists or awkward bolts. Everyone's eyes were blue. What affected me most was their un-wavering calm. I would look up from these pamphlets at my mother, sitting at the other end of the kitchen table smoking furiously, making piles of different bills and lists and papers, her kinetic anger trembling with its own life in her hands. My mother's anger at everyone and everything possessed her like a demon, making her life, as she herself often said, a living hell. She was probably aware, at times, what effect it had on ours, but most of the time she was too busy dealing with the tragedies that haunted our family or too busy stalking her own luminous sad-ness to ever sit down and speak with these demons.

Often, the pamphlets quoted verses from the Bible. These,

too, were almost always about forgiveness and love, peace, and eternal joy. This was about as close as I got to actually reading the Bible. I did try reading it at one point, after finding a King James Version in the basement. Starting with Genesis, I decided to try, as one of the pamphlets suggested, reading a page a day for a year. I got to the first string of "begat"s and that ended that project. Meanwhile, what I had read seemed a peculiar story. Why would God pick on the snake like that? And why were women made as what seemed like an afterthought? And why did everyone forever and ever have to suffer because of someone else's mistake, a mistake that, to me, didn't really seem so terrible after all? Though I'd heard that many people believed all of this was something that truly happened, surely those people would have to be discounted as idiots. All I had to do was stand outside on the front lawn, listening to the complex screams of neighborhood children and to the vast songs of the birds, to simply *know* it couldn't have happened in such a way. But then why *did* so many people believe this? And how did Jesus fit into it? From what I could understand about him, he seemed a decent sort of fellow, so why did they kill him? And why (because I'd just been reading about it in history class) did people do something as horrible as the Crusades in his name? And back in Northern Ireland, all that mess, why did that have to happen?

And yet I still longed desperately to believe. How could I cross that line? Did God exist? I conducted experiments in my room. Sitting Indian style on my carpet, I'd not so much ask as announce, "God, if you exist, prove it to me." Sometimes I'd qualify this, suggesting he (and he was always a he) do something like perhaps change the color of the carpet, or maybe make the family dog, who'd recently died, appear panting and wagging in front of me. I wanted the resounding silence following my questions to be the answer, the proof that I didn't have to waste my time wondering about such things anymore. Yet I also wanted so badly all that peace, all that joy and love.

At night I would lie in bed and pretend I was a saint. Often, I was simply an egomaniac, but that didn't matter. In my fantasy life, I learned what it felt like to have infinite patience and wisdom. I healed the sick, especially the grotesquely sick, and helped the poor, especially the poor no one else noticed, and especially the ones who lived in terror of despots. I read books about the Holocaust and imagined how graceful I would have been, that I withstood oppression with such nobility that the Nazis were forced to stop in their tracks. In Vietnam and Cambodia and amid the famines of Africa, I was there, too, helping the lost and injured and sad. In my real life, I hated myself for being petty and shallow, because, try as I might, I could only manage my transmutation into benign understanding for moments at a time. Acts of charity — these I only seemed to manage with animals, and even with them, whom I loved so much, I was often experimentally cruel. And the humans immediately around me, they had griefs far subtler than abject poverty and leprosy, sorrows far too near and familiar, and all I could do was flee.

VINCENT van Gogh, in his letters to his brother Theo, outlined a life filled with the tangible. Vincent loved to look, to touch, to smell and taste the world about him. Most of all, he loved to look and then *feel,* with his hands grasping the charcoal or brush, what he had just seen. His hands roamed all over his mind, trying to decipher the different grains of thought and emotion, the thin line between the actual and the imagined, between light and the things he saw with light. Though he never lived to hear of either wave or particle theories of light, Vincent under-stood that one doesn't just simply "see" a chair or table, but rather that one's eyes are actually caressed by the light that bounces off the object. Color, while being the most visible thing we can know about a tree, is also created by that part of light that the tree has cast off. The tree absorbs all other light waves of color, welcomes them as part of itself: the green we see is the negative, the re-flected reality it wants no part of. Where its definition of itself ends, our definition of it is just beginning.

Vincent often mentioned to his brother what he called a long-ing for the old, old story. The first time I read this, as a freshman in college, I had no idea he was referring to the story of Jesus. But I'd only just taken up writing poetry, and something about the sadness of his longing pricked at me. At that time, I was just discovering the world of writing, and it was the religion I'd been searching for all my life. That even such a short phrase as written by Vincent van Gogh could elicit such ineffable feelings in me seemed miraculous. I'd spent most of my childhood using the small tactile details of the world as a way of escaping the world: how easy to separate myself from the shame and misery of certain moments by suddenly appreciating the texture of the carpet a doctor paced on, or the dewlike drops forming on the glass of water in front of my angry mother, its reflected rim a hoop of light quivering on the table.

Writing offered a way to take these small observations and transform them into a way of entering the world, a way of using language as the slow tear in the fabric I'd been wrapping myself up in. My own particular tool was language, but I loved art of all kinds, particularly visual art. The concept of time seemed at the heart of all the arts. Art, to me, was anything that brought you into the present moment, the nameless now that keeps dying and being reborn over and over and over. That the present moment should be so nameless, so inexpressible, I believed was the fundamental truth of art, and I defined beauty as the thing left over from the effort of trying to name it. The painter Robert Henri said it best in a quote that, during the height of my artistic evangelism, I learned by heart: *There are moments in our lives, there are moments in a day, when we seem to see beyond the usual. Such are the moments of our greatest happiness. Such are the moments of our greatest wisdom. If one but could recall his vision by some sort of sign. It was in this hope that the arts were invented. Signposts on the way to what may be. Signposts toward greater knowledge.*

My senior year in college I decided to take a course titled "The Bible as Literature." I took it because of the "literature" part of the title. In my endless quest for metaphors, I thought it might help my writing. The first assignment, naturally enough, was to read Genesis. I admit I only skimmed the begats. By this time I knew enough about anthropology, ancient myths, and other world religions to recognize Genesis as a good story. For a few years previous I'd been dabbling in Eastern religion, with a little Western philosophy thrown in as well. More and more, I came to see that, just as with art, the essence of the religious moment lay within the "now" moment, and that the heinous clichés of the world were born in the belief that you could capture this moment. Once you judged, once you decided, you were closed off, locked into misinterpretations of the past and misapprehensions of the future. The more I looked at it, the more religion looked like art.

As we read more of the Old Testament, I was seized by a great crisis. The closer I read, the more shocked I was by my own previous ignorance of what was going on in the Bible. I guess I'd always thought it was all about love and joy and peace. The violence and anger of the Old Testament terrified me, but the real terror lay in my having to acknowledge that the culture I lived in was based, in large part, upon this violent saga, a story as unfair as it was unforthcoming. That so many generations upon generations of people, that people living today, took this work to be the literal truth deeply disturbed me. How could one be happy with such tautology, to simply be "told" the meaning of everything, never allowed to question it? And the entire drama of the story was based on God's will — all those humans forced into their roles — for it was God who hardened people's hearts, God who closed their eyes against the truth, God who selected only a chosen few, leaving the rest to annihilation or worse. What could the purpose of life be if it was already laid out in such monotonous script?

EARLY in the Christian era, Philo of Alexandria changed the course of history by being one of the first philosophers to undertake and, most important, to write about an allegorical exegesis of the Hebrew Scripture. Up until the time of Philo, the text of the Scripture was a kind of property, controlled by the religious officials. The text itself was mysterious to those who could not read, and faith was contained in the act of believing the stories. It was a very physical, very visceral kind of belief, one that contended that the path to salvation lay with your ability to follow ritual and to control your body. Philo, a Jew, however, read the Bible stories as allegorical. He wrote at length about the possibility that spirit and matter were separated, and that belief was an act of the mind, not simply of the body. You could perform rituals till the very end, but none of that mattered if you didn't believe with your head and heart, if you didn't actually think.

Philo inserted a new dimension into the whole concept of

belief. "Truth," as he saw it, didn't exist in the stories themselves, in the words on the page, nor in the black-and-white world of absolute faith, but in the process of using the wit and judgment and intellect given to us by God in interpreting these words. In a sense, Philo was the first deconstructionist. Meaning, for Philo, unlike many of his contemporaries, occurred not on set planes, but only in the shift between these planes. Later, of course, those different planes were all too firmly established, and rather than think for yourself, you could only move between meanings rigidly defined by the church. Philo himself, freely interpreting with only his instinct and education to guide him, would have been seen as a heretic during any number of inquisitions, despite the fact that it was his philosophies that set the groundwork for them. Surely he could never have foreseen that once people were able to move past literal methods of judging what was to become the Bible, they would then cast their abstract *ideas* about the Bible in do-or-die terms, become willing to torture and kill those who did not accept their ideas of what the Bible *meant*.

NOT surprisingly, the information that impressed me most in the Old Testament had been the use of time. If the garden of Eden was timeless, then linear history began with the Fall. The Old Testament set up a very particular story, charted an inexorable course. Within this history, which was one type of linear time, or narrative, there was a second story with an even more refined sense of linear time, and this was the story of the Covenant. On the simplest level, the Covenant was a deal made between God and the Jews. At the beginning of this deal, it was promised that once the narrative ran its course, once the string of prophecies came true, God would end history and bring his people to the promised land. This end was, paradoxically, to be a return to the beginning state, to a timeless, or eternal, paradise. As I understood it, this made time in the Bible cyclical as well as linear.

By sheer luck, I was reading Gabriel García Marquez's *One Hundred Years of Solitude* at the same time I was reading the New Testament. If my history of religion bashing prevented me from a full marveling at the narrative and artistic genius behind the story of the Bible, I was at least free to marvel at how García Marquez intermeshed cyclical with linear time, showing through images of magic realism (images that would be defined as miraculous in the Bible) that we could always be in the "now," but also that the string of nows moved inevitably forward. Death, after all, was the one now moment that brought the inner and the outer lives together: even if you've denied every now moment in your life, you are still moving forward toward that final, inevitable moment. García Marquez did this again and again with images: a bedroom untouched by time even as the house fell into decrepitude around it, the blind Ursula able to act as if she saw simply by knowing routines (time) so well. This same Ursula, the matriarch of the family, could also symbolically lift herself out of time, lift herself out of habits others were caught in, and find objects such as wedding rings others thought irrevocably lost. García Marquez exemplified the paradox of cyclical and linear time with Ursula. The Bible did it with Jesus.

As a poet, I was struck by the sheer genius of Jesus as a narrative device, Jesus as the ultimate paradox. No wonder, I thought, this story has survived with such force, no wonder it has compelled so many. Again, it was the use of time that grabbed me. Of course, there were Jesus' sermons and parables themselves, which were beautiful and attractive for their gentle strength and wisdom, but I could find any number of similar stories and sayings anywhere else I chose to look. It was the way Jesus died that tied it all together, that brought poetic force to his teachings. In particular, it was the things Jesus said on the cross as he died that, once I turned my whole life's experience toward interpreting these words, astounded me. In Luke, when Jesus says, "Father, forgive them, they know not what they do," a way to approach this utterance is to look at what he does not say. He doesn't say, "Father, forgive them because soon they'll understand what they've done and they'll be sorry." This type of reasoning for forgiveness depends upon the passage of time: in a future moment, people will be forced to relive the past and have their present moment forever sullied by that past. He doesn't say, "Father, forgive them because they are too stupid to understand what's going on and need to be pitied." To say this would be to say that humans are incapable of awareness because of a lack or deficit; rather, they know not what they do because they are trapped in the present moment and so can't understand the historical significance of their actions. And he doesn't say, "Father, forgive them because they'll be judged later anyway." This would imply a purely apocalyptic sense of time: living a string of now moments isolated from each other by stupidity, as opposed to a string of now moments linked by awareness. If you believe your life's meaning and value will be decided in the future, independent of what you do or suffer now, then there is no possibility of having your present life acquire meaning through being aware of that future, for that decision, unlinked to the now, could only be haphazard and incomprehensible.

What Jesus does say is "Father, forgive them, for they know not what they do." This implies that while the present moment may be incomprehensible, there is still the possibility of forgiveness, which would instill meaning and order not just to that single moment of future forgiveness, but would also instill meaning into all past and present moments, even those moments that were lived in doubt and chaos.

This last type of living in time is crucial to the concepts of forgiveness and redemption so significant to Christianity. If the Father represents the eternal, then his ability to forgive action created by linear time is the ultimate fusion of cyclical and linear time. When Jesus says, in John, "It is finished," I don't think he means just his life or his crusade. It is the end of the Old Testament sense of history: the prophecy has come to pass, and the violent cause-and-effect type of history embodied in the Old Testament is over: a new sense of time is now in place, a sense of time as both eternally present and eternally changing. All these incredibly complex ideas embedded in a few sentences. This terrified me.

But obviously the old sense of history, of violent and unjust cause and effect, wasn't over with the Crucifixion. If anything, the church itself became responsible for a great deal more violence. But those things *could* be changed, I believed, at least on the personal level, by acting with compassion and unconditional love. History itself would remain in place, as violent as ever, but small transcendent acts of personal dignity and grace could be performed regardless. In the face of chaos, one had to act as if order and meaning were possible, despite the fact that one could never be absolutely sure: the tangible miracles of the carpet's changing color or the resurrected dog were not going to be the guidelines of success. Rather, I had to use a much more abstract, internal gauge of spiritual success, recognizing all the while the possibility that I might simply be fooling myself. I recognized in this process exactly the same pattern as attempting to capture something in words or on a canvas, knowing all along that one will ultimately fail to produce an objective, final, and fully satisfying definition of beauty. I knew the moments in art where I was convinced I had produced something beautiful were not only the moments in which I was most likely wrong, but that the whole notion of being "convinced" was itself the seat of the problem. If paintings and poems were the signposts in art that reminded you again and again of your needs and beliefs rather than letting you get sucked into the abyss of your failures, then the words and deeds of Jesus could work the same way.

When Jesus was on the cross, depending on which Gospel you're reading, he said several different things. One of them is a question. "My God, my God, why hast thou forsaken me?" Except he doesn't even really ask that — in the two Gospels it's present in, it's presented first in another language, *"Eloi, Eloi, lama sabachthani," Eloi* coming from the Aramaic, or, *"Eli, Eli, lama sabachthani," Eli* coming from the Hebrew. The "original" is offered so we readers can fathom why those near him misunderstand and think he's calling for Elijah. There is more written on this one verse in the Gospels than perhaps on any other. "Is Jesus quoting the Twenty-second Psalm?" the interpreters ask. "Is it instructive: is he questioning God so that we can see that it's acceptable to have moments of doubt?" It's when I read people writing about the Bible that I feel the most alien from religion; and also when I feel the most sorry for us all. Many interpreters have gone to great pains to prove that Jesus' question is answered: after all, it's followed in Luke's Gospel with "Father, into thy hands I commend my spirit." Surely that statement right there shows he was answered, doesn't it? And yet, in Matthew and Mark, Jesus' last living sound is neither question nor comment, but a cry, a loud cry (Mark 15:37). Even this "cry" has been under intense scrutiny, some writers going so far as to call it a

"voice," and declaring it wasn't a wail, as anyone else being crucified might let out, but actually a cry of victory. As if it would be
too much to know that Jesus' last words were wordless, a cry of
deep sorrow and pain. The need to know, the need to have it all
be all right, to all make sense.

What hasn't been written on very much is the fact that such a
crucial moment in Christianity centers on translation. This is one
of a very few moments of translation in the Bible, one of a very
few moments when alien words are included as part of the whole
meaning. I view this as being about how sometimes we can't understand each other and need someone to intercede for us. The
final truth doesn't exist in one parcel of words or the other, but in
both, and more importantly, in the space between the words, in
that brief moment after you read the foreign words but before
they are explained.

Even after discovering the Bible, I didn't want to Believe, not
with a capital *B*. I didn't want to turn into the type of person I'd
regarded as stupid my entire life. But there it was again: was I just
being trapped by my own history, my own inability to let go of
the past? It was as if I were sitting back on my childhood carpet,
the smell of tomato sauce coming from the kitchen, the sounds of
scraping pots, as I tried to appeal myself into a position of belief.
Wasn't I supposed to just take the plunge now, that proverbial
leap? Was it even a matter of will at all? I spent days lying on my
bed in my college dorm, staring out the window at the gutter
hanging down from the roof in the foreground, the top of an oak
tree in the middle ground where large flocks of noisy starlings
congregated each dusk, and the sky beyond.

I was taking chemistry at the time, and in lab each small
group was handed little vials of an unknown substance. Our task
was to determine what it was. In order to do this, we went

through a series of tests, tests that were really questions: What is its density? What is its melting point? Will it oxidate? Some of the questions were useful to ask; some were not. If you had a mineral, asking its boiling point was meaningless, but stumbling upon the question of its fracture angle unlocked everything. Once we found the correct set of questions to ask, we gradually uncovered the chemical structure and were eventually able to supply our professor with the substance's name. He, of course, knew all along what it was. The substance was itself the answer: our job was to find the right questions.

TOWARD the end of writing my memoir, *The Autobiography of a Face,* in 1994, I realized I was becoming disgustingly, though perhaps not surprisingly, self-involved. Bitter and jealous, I stock-piled my own list of personal grievances. In particular, I was jealous of a woman who had cervical cancer: I thought she got to have all the "benefits" of a hard experience but didn't have to suffer any permanent visible scars. She was beautiful and had just fallen in love with a friend of mine. I felt ugly and had just broken up from a traumatic affair. Able to see that I was turning into something I didn't want to be, I kept trying to "get a new outlook." Eventually, after realizing there was no way to think my way out of this depressing state, I decided on real-world action. I called up a hospice and volunteered to help dying patients write their memoirs. It was an act of pure ego: I thought I would finally be able to view myself as that kind, loving person I always so wanted to be. As it turned out, most of the patients were too debilitated either to want or to be able to write, or even dictate, their stories. Most of the time I spent volunteering was spent sitting or standing next to a bed, offering what the hospice called "a ministry of presence." I held their hands, I stroked their foreheads. Sometimes I rubbed their feet, which was difficult because it is true: the body dies in increments. The feet often go first, and what I had to take in my hands was often scaly and flaccid. I always thought of Christ washing the feet of his apostles. For me, it was pure symbol. For them, it was kindness, perhaps some small relief.

After several weeks on the inpatient ward, I noticed a curious thing. Many of the nurses, aides, and other volunteers were in the habit of bringing men they were interested in to the hospice to meet patients of whom they were particularly fond. Ostensibly this was so the boyfriend could see part of his girlfriend's life, but as soon as he left there would be a great conspiratorial rush to the patient's bedside. "So what do you think of him?" In the past, the dying have always been assigned great mystical powers of truth-saying, and in the way my new lovelorn coworkers hung on the patients' slow, painful words, words sometimes meted out a breathless syllable at a time, the same belief lived on. They would lean over the patients, in a ward always overheated and overlit, asking their questions with the belief that there is a final bottom to a person, that we can hit bottom and distinguish a person fully if only we throw the penny down the well often enough, and that it is only the dying who are unencumbered enough to tell us how.

FRANK was a patient in the hospice who had been dying for two years, though he had been told dozens of times that only months were left. Everyone on the ward had a chance to get to know him quite well. Near the end he was on four grams of morphine a day; four *milligrams* is more than most people could take. He was like a man underwater, all his responses slowed almost to a halt. Often, he would fall asleep in midconversation, even midgesture, freezing in place, and you had to wait for him to wake back up. My friend Phoebe, his nurse, brought him blue irises one day, and also her boyfriend. Frank held the unopened irises one at a time and flicked at them with his forefinger and thumb, ever so slowly, to make them open. It was a trick his mother had taught him, and she had insisted they must be flicked twice. They opened, coming to life, so slowly, so very slowly, yet quicker than it took Frank to finish his second flick.

After the boyfriend was sent out for coffee, Phoebe leaned over Frank's bed. I was holding onto his feet, which were hot from being under the blanket I'd just pulled back off them. "Frank, what do you think?" Slowly, he told her, "I don't want to give you bad news." "What, Frank, tell me, you didn't like him?" Frank held his arm up to look at his watch, and then actually fell asleep in that position, his arm held up in front of his face, his body wrapped up in a blue cotton blanket. Phoebe didn't see that he'd fallen asleep. "Frank, you can tell me, is it bad?" Then she realized and started to laugh. She looked up at me and said, "Frank is always turning my dialogues into monologues." Then the boyfriend walked back in. He seemed a decent enough person, carrying a streaked brown cardboard carrier with three particularly bright Styrofoam cups. It had been raining all day, and water dripped off the coat he hung on the door. He didn't say anything. The three of us sat there, waiting for Frank, waiting for him to wake up and turn Phoebe's monologue back into a dialogue, waiting for him there with his irises, holding our unnaturally white cups of coffee.

Love's Alchemy

bell hooks

CHILDREN growing up in the old South often heard the words "brought up on the Book." This saying was used when folks talked about styles of parenting and whether they were informed by close, vigilant reading of the Bible. Folks who held the Book to be sacred often quoted lengthy passages to affirm their actions. I was raised to be a child of the Book. During the morning service at our beloved Baptist church I would read the Scripture for the children's offering as the organist played music to accompany the sound of my voice softly speaking words from our most sacred text. As part of my missionary service growing up, I went door to door reading the Scripture to those who could not read or write. I still remember my profound shock when I was a freshman in college and saw in the course list a class called "The Bible as Literature." And though I went to this class once, the cheerful mockery of the text made it impossible for me to remain. It was still the "Good Book" in my eyes, to be loved and cherished above all other books.

Over time I began to read the religious texts of other faiths and found in them great poetry, sacred words, as well as guides for living. I placed them not above the "Good Book" but alongside it. While my relationship to organized, institutionalized Christianity has changed, my devotion to "the Book" remains. During meditations I tend to choose passages from the Bible to guide my spiritual reflections. One of my favorites is the passage from the First Epistle of John, chapter 4, verse 18: "There is no fear in love; but perfect love casteth out fear: because fear hath torment. He that feareth is not made perfect in love." From childhood on, this passage has enchanted me because of the repeated use of the word "perfect." For some time I thought of this word only in relation to being without fault or defect. Taught to believe that this understanding of what it means to be perfect was always out of human reach, that we were of necessity essentially human because we were not perfect, always bound by the mystery of the body — by our limitations — this call to know a perfect love disturbed me. It seemed a worthy calling but impossible. That is until I looked for a deeper, more complex understanding of the word "perfect" and found a definition that emphasized the will "to refine."

Suddenly, my passage was illuminated. Love as a process that has been refined, alchemically altered as it moves from stage to stage, is that "perfect love" that can cast out fear. The word "cast" has this wonderful double function. Not only does it evoke images of a process of shedding or molting, it also suggests an element of spontaneous change. Hence, the uses of the word "cast" suggest that casting out fear is merely a by-product, rather than the purpose, of the loving process. As we love, fear necessarily leaves. Contrary to the notion that one must work to attain perfection, this outcome does not have to be struggled for — it happens. It is the gift perfect love offers.

To receive the gift, we must first understand that "there is no fear in love." This declaration militates against contemporary cul-

tural assumptions that socialize us to believe that anxiety, inse-
curity, and fear are "natural" responses when one desires to love or
be loved. In *Enchantment and Discernment* José Ortega y Gasset
suggests that the way we love outwardly mirrors our inner state of
being: "Since love is the most delicate and total act of a soul, it will
reflect the state and nature of the soul. If the individual is not
sentient, how can his love be sentient? If he is not profound, how
can his love be deep? As one is, so is his love." If one begins with
this premise, then if the heart is full of fear, it is that condition that
will manifest when one strives to love. Remaining attached to fear
will disrupt and interfere with the will to love. If we think of love
as the convergence of feeling and action, then it is impossible to
feel love even as one is simultaneously trapped by fear. This state of
entrapment usually leads to a state of emotional paralysis that
renders all movement from feeling to action impossible.

Though written at a time when fear was not deeply associated
with the act of loving, the declaration "There is no fear in love"
prophetically interrogates. It demands that we question the place
of fear in our lives. Everyone longs to know love. And yet we cling
to fear. For many of us our childhood longing for love, for a
world that would nurture our well-being holistically, has never
been fulfilled. Fear always militates against trust in love.

Cultures of domination tend to rely on the cultivation of fear
as a way to ensure obedience. In its rhetoric such a society makes
much of love and says little of the pervasiveness of fear. Yet we are
all so terribly afraid most of the time. Fear is the prevailing cultural force that upholds structures of domination. It promotes the
desire for separation, the desire not to be known. If we are taught
that safety lies always with sameness, then "difference" of any
kind will appear as threat. No wonder Martin Luther King
evoked this passage from 1 John in his essay "Strength to Love,"

raising the question: "In these days of catastrophic change and calamitous uncertainty, is there any man who does not experience the depression and bewilderment of crippling fear, which, like a nagging hound of hell, pursues our every footstep?" Seeing fear as the underlying emotional catalyst for the perpetuation of racism, King urged the world to consider the power of love as a means to transform structures of domination. His faith in the power of love to transform was rooted in the understanding that imperialism, colonialism, and white supremacy all rely on the fear felt for the unknown "other" to sustain themselves. Raising the question of whether or not love has a "relationship to our modern fear of war, economic displacement and racial injustice," King insisted:

> Hate is rooted in fear, and the only cure for fear-hate is love. Our deteriorating international situation is shot through with the lethal darts of fear. . . . In these turbulent, panic-stricken days we are once more reminded of the judicious words of old, "Perfect love casteth out fear." Not arms, but love, understanding, and organized goodwill can cast out fear. Only disarmament, based on good faith, will make mutual trust a living reality.

King's insistence on the primacy of love was often mocked by critics who believed militant intervention would create more immediate change than loving. They were wrong. Love of justice has empowered people to work for and achieve progressive social-change strategies.

Despite its efficacy, the simple call to love without fear has not been fully heard and realized because we live in a culture that teaches us fear from birth. That it is "normal" to be fearful is imprinted on practically everyone's cultural psyche from birth. In tense times, fears of abandonment help sustain regimes of coercive authoritarian control. In her poem "Litany For Survival" Audre Lorde shares that "when we are loved we are afraid love will vanish." Living with such fear, we are afraid to love even as we long to be loved. Movements for self-recovery, whether they take the form of more sophisticated psychoanalysis or basic self-help therapy, all strive to restore to us the belief that life is not to be feared and that we can connect fully with others only when we let go of fear.

In 1 John we are encouraged to find comfort in the belief that "perfect love casteth out fear." That comfort is suggested by the word "but." While we are told, "There is no fear in love," embedded in the passage "But perfect love casteth out fear" is the assumption that even if fear exists it can be released by the experience of perfect love. The alchemy of perfect love is such that it offers to the beloved and/or lover a love that is able to vanquish fear. That which is rendered separate or other through fear is made whole through perfect love. It is this perfect love that is redemptive — that can, like the intense heat of alchemical fire, burn away impurities and leave the soul free. Fear is the impurity, and perfect love undoes its hold on our hearts.

A dimension of perfect love, then, must be that it remains always unconditional. The reassurance that we will always be loved irrespective of our behavior means that abandonment need not be feared, for it will never happen. Were everyone in our culture to be free of the fear of abandonment, we could constructively challenge and eradicate systems of domination that prey on such fears. Indeed, this passage from 1 John counters the logic of white supremacist capitalist patriarchal thinking that condones coercion and as a consequence promotes the cultivation of fear in the powerless by the powerful as the easiest means to inspire terror and gain control.

Significantly, we are told in this passage that it is crucial that love casts out fear "because fear hath torment." These words speak directly to the persistent presence of anguish in the lives of those who are driven by fear. The practice of loving, then, is offered as the healing force that brings sustained peace. Since, as the passage concludes, "He that feareth is not made perfect in love," the challenge is to love even as one dwells in fear. For it is the practice of love that transforms. As one gives and receives love, fear is let go. Perfect love is attained through this process of refinement. As we live the understanding that "there is no fear in love," experientially witnessing that our anguish is diminished, we garner strength to enter more deeply into love's paradise. When we are able to accept that giving ourselves over to love completely restores the soul, we can be made perfect in love.

To a grave extent, the transformative power of love is not fully embraced in our society because we have come to believe that torment and anguish are our "natural" condition. This assumption is affirmed by the ongoing tragedy that prevails in modern society. In a world anguished by rampant destruction, fear seems to be the rational response to everything unfamiliar in daily life. We are all diminished by this thinking and the response it engenders.

Cultural cynicism about the meaning of love has led to utter devaluation of the art of loving. Indeed, in most of our lives the only love that is deemed significant is romantic love, and even then we are told it is rarely sustained through time. Since patriarchy has corrupted family life so that love cannot prevail in the intimacy of home, no wonder most of us do not expect to find love in the world outside. Allegiance to a facile understanding of patriarchy that sees it solely as male domination of women allows little attention to be given to the way in which patriarchal thinking encourages us all to see men as "naturally" unable to connect emotionally, as unable to give sustained nurture and care. Mainstream sexist notions of masculinity continually socialize males to see themselves as inadequate to the task of loving, and to see this as unproblematic. Indeed, much of the fear children have of being unworthy of love emerges in their relation to fathers who refuse them acknowledgment and care. Sadly, the contemporary men's movement has not yet offered to men a revolutionary feminist vision of masculinity that would restore to their lives recognition of the primacy of love, and of their power to be loving.

While I do not in any way believe women are less capable of doing violence than men, or that we are rarely violent (plenty of women are daily perpetuating acts of violence against children), it is clear that women are encouraged to learn ways of loving whether we enact them or not. Yet women are deeply complicit with the maintenance of ways of thinking that suggest it is fine for men to fail at loving, and that love is only the province of courageous women and those rare men who defy patriarchy to find their way to love. It is especially poignant that the passage "He that feareth is not made perfect in love" uses the masculine pronoun, for collective male fear of love is endangering all our lives and the well-being of the planet.

To return to love, to know perfect love, we must be willing to surrender the will to power. It is this understanding that makes this passage from 1 John so prophetic and revolutionary for our times. We cannot know love if we remain unable to surrender our attachment to power, if any feeling of vulnerability strikes terror in our hearts. As our cultural awareness of the ways love has been taken from us gains recognition, our anguish intensifies, but so does our yearning. The space of our lack is also the space of possibility. As we yearn, we make ourselves ready for the love that is coming to us, as gift, as promise, as earthly paradise.

The Good Enough News

Lisa Shea

A S a child, listening to my mother read to my sisters and me from the New Testament, I tried to care about the people in the stories, who were lame or leprous or blind, who ate locusts and raw fish, who didn't have television or telephones or toilets, who were homeless or lunatic or possessed. I pictured these Bible people, even the famous ones like Mary Magdalene and John the Baptist, unwashed, dressed in rags, their hair hanging down infested and uncombed. My eight-year-old body shuddered, because of course they must have smelled bad, and what about their teeth, if they even had any!

It seemed a sore test of my belief in God that he could love these ancient, unkempt people; that he had picked them to be born and live and die among and not us who washed and drank milk and went to church on Sunday in America in 1963. I thought it was a waste of the Savior of Mankind, an error on God's part to have sent his only son to earth so early on, before we really needed Christ to save us from Khrushchev and Castro, and Richard

Nixon, a man whose hatred of President Kennedy I knew made him evil.

Other aspects of the Bible vexed and bewildered me as my sisters and I lay sprawled on our parents' three-legged bed,* hearing the stories in their entirety for the first time. There were the Pharisees, who tried to trick Jesus at every turn. I had no idea who the Pharisees were, but the word made them sound like phony piranhas or farcical parasites. There were the high priests, whose identity also was obscure to me. Why were they in synagogues instead of churches? I didn't know there weren't any churches because there was, as yet, no Church. So the high priests came off as bogus, a pack of holy lowlifes.

God the Father was a problem because he was too much like my own father: everywhere and all-knowing, without bounds. He was the angry, billowing face in the clouds commanding us to love, honor, and obey. If you sinned, it was not only against humanity but against him, and he could strike you sideways with lightning, strike you dead. I very much wanted to be saved, but not by this mad God. I'd hide around my house and yard, even though I knew he could see me and see inside me, that he could read my thoughts. I still think God the Father can read my thoughts, that there is a celestial listening post inside my head. No amount of psychotherapy has cured me of this vestige of early belief, this faith-induced paranoia.

God the Holy Ghost was okay, beautiful and benevolent, but

* In place of the broken fourth leg was a stack of books. The only title I remember is William Shirer's *The Rise and Fall of the Third Reich.* I had looked at the book's grisly pictures over and over, trying (and failing, as with the Bible stories now) to fathom their meaning in the world.

he was abstract, a sacred, birdlike creature who symbolized peace and other imponderables, things that could never come to exist on our sorry planet. In the days before he is crucified, Jesus tells his apostles that even though he is leaving them, the Holy Ghost, whom he calls the Comforter and the Spirit of Truth, is coming to take his place. This information is supposed to cheer the apostles, but you can tell they are taking it badly, that they want Jesus, a man among them, and not some replacement little white dove.

Despite my difficulties with the Bible stories, over the weeks at bedtime, as my mother read the Gospel of Matthew in her lively speech-and-drama-major voice, I fell in love with God's son. Before, I had thought of him as the dead man on the cross with a gash in his side, a loincloth lashed to his hips, and a wicked crown of thorns ringing his bloodied head. In the snatches of stories I had heard from the nuns at school and the priests at Mass, he had come across as slightly scary and creepy, maybe insane.

Now, when I looked at the crucifix hanging over my parents' bed, what I noticed was Christ's near nakedness, the sinewy plane of his ribs, the elegant shape of his inclined head. His whole posture was one of charged physical surrender. He was still dead, but he was sexy. In this way, Jesus became the prototype for crushes I would later develop on a succession of other deceased historical and artistic figures — Chopin, Abraham Lincoln, Nietzsche, Oscar Wilde, Keats.

Beginning with Christ, these men — with whom I craved impossible communion — had in common an irresistible combination of melancholic looks, tragic lives, and a knack for producing works of genius (in Christ's case, think of the miracles!). My penchant for these necrophiliac romances was supported by my upbringing in a home that was Irish, Catholic, patriarchal, violent, alcoholic. I thought I could never love a real man, but it might be possible to love a dead man who was larger than life.

Of these fantasy men, Christ was by far the most handsome. In the popular renderings of the day, he had long wavy hair, an aquiline nose, and soulful — our mother would have called them bedroom — eyes. His was a portrait of masculine beauty and serenity, a face radiating quiet, unthreatening authority. What kind of man was this, I wondered, who, unlike my own father, was brilliant but not bullying, powerful but not paranoid, handsome but not arrogant, sexy but not sadistic? At night in the dark, in the room I shared with my younger sister, I kissed my framed Sacred Heart Auto League picture of Jesus (given to me by my grandfather, who was a member) over and over.

Like the apostles, I wanted Christ to be with me, my savior-lover made flesh. Then, as my mother finished the Gospel According to Matthew and began reading us Mark in late November, President Kennedy was shot. Somehow, my crush on Jesus Christ got mixed up with my new crush on our dead president. I fantasized that JFK was Christ with a Harvard accent and a haircut and gleaming white teeth, and that he had died to save us from the Russians. Their leader, the living Khrushchev, already was satanic, with his bloated body, his ugly red face, his awful temper, and his shiny bald head. Who else was Lee Harvey Oswald but Khrushchev's assassinating minion?

Through the terrible days and weeks after the killing, my mother read on, finishing Mark and beginning Luke, but her voice wasn't lively; it sounded heavy and tired. Sometimes, she would stop and cry, and we'd cry with her, thinking about our murdered president. She'd sit, not reading, and sip quietly from her "Coffee with Kennedy" cup, a souvenir from her volunteer work on the 1960 campaign. I was upset that Jackie and Caroline and John had to leave the White House so that Johnson and his dowdy wife and largish, oafish daughters could move in. President Johnson didn't seem evil, but he was vulgar, a big-eared ham from Texas with barroom, not bedroom, eyes.

By the following spring, as my mother read us the Gospel According to John (in a voice that had regained some of its fine theatricality), my older sister and I had discovered the Beatles. Every day we'd come home from school — we were latchkey kids — turn on the radio in the dining room to WPGC-AM, LOUD, and dance to Beatles songs. I worked out a theory that each of the Gospel writers was like one of the Beatles. Mark was lively like Paul; Matthew was quieter like George; Luke was lovable like Ringo; and John was just like John, smart, harsh, inscrutable. My older sister's favorite Beatle was Paul, whose sunniness I found a little boring. My favorite was George, who was lanky like Christ and who had those necrotic good looks. (My younger sister, who was five, wasn't into the Beatles; she liked Dwayne Spedden, who was also five and lived next door with his cousins.)

Comparing John, Paul, George, and Ringo to Matthew, Mark, Luke, and John pointed to a huge change — a conversion, really — in my thinking about the New Testament. Now a seasoned listener, I had developed a secret passion for the stories that early on had so repulsed me. They were as gruesome and baffling as ever, but through some mysterious confluence of my mother's engaging voice, my galloping crush on Jesus Christ, the violent death of our president, and finally putting faces (the Beatles'!) on the powerful voices of the Gospel narrators, these seductive, hair-raising tales had become real.

As my mother began reading the Acts of the Apostles early in the summer, I felt the stirrings of my faith. I was especially interested in the story of Saul, who fell down blinded by the light of God on the road to Damascus to round up some Christians. The passage in our 1960s Chain-Reference Bible read: "And suddenly there shined round about him a light from heaven: And he fell to the earth, and heard a voice saying unto him, Saul, Saul, why persecutest thou me?" And then, a few lines later, Saul, still lying on the ground, asks, "Lord, what wilt thou have me to do?"

The idea of a bad man becoming a good, even a holy man, was astonishing (and suspect) to me. I tried to imagine something like this happening to Khrushchev or Castro or Nixon, or my father, but their cases seemed so hardened, completely hopeless. I was also drawn to the nature of Saul's conversion* — sudden, violent, without warning (like an accident, like death) — which so satisfied my love of drama, of unexpected, untamed things.

Walking home from school, I'd practice falling down, struck blind by goodness, forever changed. Standing up, I'd squint my eyes hard and see how far I could walk virtually sightless, saying over and over as if in a trance, "I see men as trees, walking." This was my favorite line of Scripture, spoken by the blind man in Mark 8:24 before his sight is fully restored. I had no idea what it meant, but it sounded like poetry, obscure and surreal, unlike the rest of the Bible with its simple — if profound — parable-rife prose, which had taken me so long to like.

Toward the end of the summer, our New Testament gatherings on my parents' bed became more sporadic. I am pretty sure my mother had begun reading us the Bible as a stay against the

---

* In the drawings I saw of this event, Saul was invariably pictured having fallen from his horse at the moment of conversion. Even though the Bible made no mention of a horse, the equine detail greatly enhanced my obsession with the story. Those days, the only thing I wanted to be besides Christ's lover was a horse.

Cold War scares of the early sixties: bomb shelters, Cuban Missile Crisis, air-raid drills, Bay of Pigs. That and the more personal hell of her deteriorating marriage to my increasingly volatile father. Maybe she thought the Bible would guide us or help us or even save us from all the public and private terribleness abroad in the world and in our own unhappy house.

Merely to be alive on the outskirts of the nation's capital at that time was to experience a daily rehearsal for Armageddon, for a horrific end to the world as we knew it. Why else did I so diligently study the fallout maps my father collected, the ones showing in a widening radius from ground zero (the White House) the number of people expected to be killed or wounded in a nuclear attack. Where we lived, six miles out, there would be no survivors.

Paul's dramatic conversion fed my already apocalypse-trained imagination in a way none of the other Bible events did. It was hard to think of what story I might need or want after this. And then, around the beginning of the new school year, the readings ceased altogether. I'm pretty sure my mother stopped reading us the New Testament not because the world had become a safer place but because she was miserable and exhausted, worn out from the chaos that ruled our home.*

Quickly, my crush on Jesus Christ ended, not to mention my memory of his words and deeds, his divine miracles. God's love might be everlasting, but mine was fickle. I'd look at my Sacred Heart Auto League picture of Christ and wonder what it was I ever saw in him. Saul stayed with me a while longer, but apart

---

* In another year, my mother and sisters and I would leave that house for a high-rise apartment building that overlooked a synagogue, which I began to attend with a Spanish-speaking Jewish family I befriended.

from his conversion from Saul to Paul, I forgot the rest of his story — his arrival in Damascus, where he remained blind for three days, his peripatetic preaching and his writings, his pillarship, along with Peter, of the early church.

That winter, for my ninth birthday, I had been given a recording of Chopin's nocturnes, and now I became infatuated with the gaunt, handsome figure on the back of the album cover. On our portable record player, I listened to the music over and over, holding the album cover to my lips the way I once had held the wallet-sized picture of Jesus. Chopin's music, with its slow, sure cadences, its ripe melancholy, made, to my hungering ears, a sacred, moody, seductive sound that I transposed right onto Chopin's long, sad face.

In the months after my mother stopped reading us the Bible, I'd see the book in my parents' bedroom, lying on the night table next to their bed, on my mother's vanity, the windowsill, on the floor, on top of my father's file cabinet. It was just another object, movable and mute, something dispensable, in the way. Occasionally, I'd pick up the book and open it to a random page, but the print was painfully small; when I tried reading, the letters jumped and twitched like Raid-sprayed black ants.

I felt sorry for the Bible, for my old love Jesus, but I was a wild-hearted girl with a huge appetite for fantasy that kept taking swift and sudden turns. My romance with Jesus Christ was intense and true and then it ended, the way each of my crushes on the dead men of all time would. It wasn't something I had control over, this feverish swell of desire followed by the next feverish swell of desire.

My main belief during the early sixties was that at any moment the world might end, that my troubled family and I would be heat-flashed by the demon Russians into glowing particles of atomic ash. The Bible's world-without-end message paled in comparison to this idée fixe that complete annihilation — no more jump rope, no more fireflies, no more Swamp Fox — was certain and nigh.

I still think about the people in the Bible. Far from feeling scorn, I envy them their living witness. What was my silly after-school mime to that? And I still want to know: Is God real? Is religion real? Can I, can anybody, be saved? The New Testament stories taught me to think on these things, even if I can't bring myself to believe, at least not in any straightforward way.

In my own (lapsed Catholic) home, instead of the New Testament, I read my five year-old son — and he reads me — animal stories from the *New York Times,* from the *Macmillan Animal Encyclopedia* and countless new and library and sidewalk and hand-me-down books. It's a stretch from the Gospel's Good News to All the News That's Fit to Print, from the greatest story ever told to sundry stories and articles about hairless moles and Curious George and gigantosauruses and Frog and Toad and baby raccoons and Muffin Mouse and housecats wandering the cargo holds of planes.

I wish I could give my son what my mother tried to give her daughters — awareness of a world that promised life everlasting. But he's inherited a large measure of my dreaming, doubting, doleful nature. Is God an animal? he wants to know. I think God is a spirit, I tell him. What kind of animal is that? he asks.

Is doubt a form of belief? For me, the answer is yes. But it is an answer without end whose authority is undermined by my eternal skepticism; belief and disbelief existing in a kind of on-going affirmation/negation of one another: I doubt, therefore I believe. I believe, therefore I doubt. Spiritually, this is as far as I've come since those Good News gatherings.

What's good about it, I'd think to myself after John the Baptist lost his head or Herod ordered all the newborns slaughtered or one of Christ's apostles cut off the ear of a Roman soldier. Then Jesus would cure a leper or feed four thousand people with seven loaves and "a few little" fishes or raise Lazarus from the dead, and I'd think, That's what's good. It wasn't anything that could ever happen to or help us, but it was still good news. Good enough.

Underdog
The Holy Spirit of Acts

Jeffrey Eugenides

I

When it comes to the Trinity, I have a favorite: the Holy Spirit. I like every scene in the Bible where this mysterious creature appears. When the prophet Joel proclaims, "And it shall come to pass afterward, that I will pour out my Spirit upon all flesh" (Joel 2:28), I get a giddy, millennial rush. When Jesus himself announces, "When he, the Spirit of truth, is come, he will guide you into all truth" (John 16:13), I give immediate assent (who can argue with the Spirit of truth?). The Spirit's attractions are like those of a cult band or unsung genius. No bumper sticker ever coaxed, "Honk if you love the Holy Ghost." Jesus gets all the attention, all the reviews, both favorable and negative. Nevertheless, according to his own promise, it should be otherwise. After the Ascension, the Holy Spirit is humanity's chief contact on earth.

One reason for the neglect (outside the Pentecostal church just down the block) is the confused portrait the Scriptures paint of the Spirit. Nobody in the New Testament seems to know what the Holy Spirit is. In the portentous early chapters of the Gospels, the Holy Spirit takes the form it does in so much Renaissance painting: that of a white dove dropping from heaven, targeting Jesus like a smart — or in this case omniscient — missile. Other times the Spirit appears in the vaguely licentious image of a "tongue of fire." Like Big Daddy in *Cat on a Hot Tin Roof,* the Holy Spirit is talked about a long time before it ever makes an entrance. Throughout the New Testament the Spirit is proclaimed, discussed, described, promised, and predicted. Finally, late in act 3 (or, more precisely, Acts 2), it happens: "And suddenly there came a sound from heaven, as of a rushing mighty wind, and it filled all the house where they were sitting. And there appeared unto them cloven tongues, like as of fire, and it sat upon each of them; And they were all filled with the Holy Ghost, and began to speak with other tongues, as the Spirit gave them utterance" (Acts 2:2–4).

The Holy Spirit turns out to be bigger than Big Daddy. The Holy Spirit is Godot — a Godot who shows up.

II

Since we're dealing with wind here, with something so indefinable and elusive that it sprouts wings one minute and tongues the next, we can aspire to no true knowledge of the Spirit. The best we can do is to intuit the Spirit through its effect on what it passes over, as we see the movement of wind in grass. Acts begins with Jesus' Ascension into heaven. In the next chapter, as consolation, the Holy Spirit arrives at Pentecost, taking up residence in the apostles and causing them to "speak with other tongues" (Acts 2:3). This is the first effect the Spirit has on humanity, and it's important to understand it. This glossolalia isn't oracular gibberish. It's a divine Berlitz Method. Under the Spirit's guidance the apostles are transformed, after just one lesson, into a cadre of precise and unnaturally concordant U.N. translators. Though all Galileans, they suddenly speak the language of "Parthians, and Medes, and Elamites, and the dwellers in Mesopotamia, and in Judea, and Cappadocia, in Pontus, and Asia, Phrygia, and Pamphylia, in Egypt, and in the parts of Libya about Cyrene, and strangers of Rome, Jews and proselytes, Cretes and Arabians" (Acts 2:9–11). The significance of all this is twofold. First, this new fluency can only bring to mind the story of the world's previous descent into cacophany. Pentecost becomes the cure for Babel. Second, and more important to the case at hand, the exhaustive list of languages makes it clear that Pentecost has less to do with the apostles' ecstatic possession by the Spirit than with the purpose of that possession, which is to enable them to speak to people they'd normally avoid like the plague.

Thus inspired and equipped, the apostles spread out over the territory. They perform miracles, proclaim Jesus as the Christ, and testify to the Resurrection. For their pains they are seized, stoned, brought before tribunals, and thrown into prison. Nevertheless, the language of Acts never lets you forget that the Holy Spirit is behind everything the apostles do. Again and again come passages such as "They chose Stephen, a man full of faith and the Holy Ghost" (6:5), or "But [Stephen], being full of the Holy Ghost" (7:54), or "Then the Spirit said unto Philip" (8:29). No other book of the New Testament mentions the Holy Spirit so often or dissolves its human actors so thoroughly.

One of the most shocking suggestions in Acts is that Jesus of Galilee was not such a hot preacher. To the contrary, after his three-year ministry, his sell-out Sermon on the Mount, and even his martyrdom, he had managed to convert, according to the accounting in Acts 1:15, "about a hundred and twenty" people. Such is the estimate, at any rate, of the "disciples" Peter first addresses in Jerusalem. (Compare that to, say, the followers of Sri Chinmoy in Southern California alone.) It is the job of the Holy Spirit to change all that. The Book of Acts tells the story of how that number grew and how the Christian Church came into existence. It maps the flow of the divine wind as it comes down from heaven and spreads out across the globe from Jew to gentile. We have to remember, of course, that this progression — from Jew to gentile — wasn't uppermost in the apostles' minds. In fact, it wasn't in their minds at all. Being Jews, and accepting Jesus as the Messiah, they see the arrival of the Spirit as a Jewish concern. This doesn't turn out to be the case, however. The Holy Spirit refuses to be contained.

"And they of the circumcision which believed were astonished, as many as came with Peter, because that on the Gentiles also was poured out the gift of the Holy Ghost. . . . Then answered Peter, Can any man forbid water, that these should not be baptized, which have received the Holy Ghost as well as we?" (10:45–47). This realization accompanies others. Once Peter accepts the gentiles, he has to rethink the entire Jewish law. "Ye know how that it is an unlawful thing for a man that is a Jew to keep company, or come unto one of another nation; but God hath showed me that I should not call any man common or unclean" (Acts 10:28).

The Holy Spirit continually amazes the apostles, even scandalizes them. Time and again they consult their new Counselor and reevaluate their opinions. They're not the only ones. Acts contains one of the most famous scenes of conversion in Western culture. In Acts 7, the apostle Stephen is stoned to death. Saul of Tarsus is on hand, "consenting unto his death" (8:1). Soon, however, Saul, like everybody else in this book, undergoes, to put it lightly, a transformation in his thinking. "And as he journeyed, he came near Damascus: and suddenly there shined round about him a light from heaven: And he fell to the earth, and heard a voice saying unto him, Saul, Saul, why persecutest thou me?" (9:3–4). The experience leaves Saul blind for days. He regains his sight only when Ananias lays hands on him, and Saul, now Paul, is filled with the Spirit, too.

So here are our first clues: whatever the Holy Spirit is, it respects no boundaries and it breaks the rules.

I I I

After the divine wind has swept onto the earth, after it has knocked Saul to the dust of the roadside, it fills his sails and brings him to Athens, where he makes an astonishing theological statement: "Ye men of Athens," Paul proclaims in Acts 17, "I perceive that in all things ye are [very religious].* For as I passed by, and beheld your devotions, I found an altar with this inscription, TO THE UNKNOWN GOD. Whom therefore ye ignorantly worship, him declare I unto you" (17:22–23).

Paul makes this address to a meeting of the Areopagus, the ancient Athenian council of elders. During the fifth and sixth centuries B.C., the Areopagus had been a body of significant judicial and legislative power, one of its chief duties being the jurisdiction of murder cases. So here, in Acts 17, the New Testament shows an uncanny ability to operate novelistically. Considering

---

* On the few occasions when I felt the King James translation of the New Testament confused the meaning of a quoted text, I have used the New Revised Standard Version instead. These instances are indicated by brackets.

the number of prison doors that slam shut throughout Acts, considering its preoccupation with the difference between secular and divine judgment, it seems only fitting that Paul, at the story's climax, should end up before the bench of a homicide court. It's the kind of thing Dickens would do: heap up scenes in jails and courtrooms, evoke chilling tribunals, cast a pall of murder in the air to bolster his theme, in this case: crime, punishment, and liberation.

From a literary standpoint it's even better than that. By the time Paul came before the Areopagus, its power was already history. We are told in Acts 17:21 that "the Athenians, and strangers which were there, spent their time in nothing else, but either to tell, or to hear some new thing." The Areopagus Paul addresses is no longer a supreme court; it's a debating society or Rotary club. Paul comes before them not as an accused criminal but as a speaker on the lecture circuit. So we have two notions going here: on the one hand, judgment and the power of the state; on the other, the crumbling of the state and its laws.

I V

Just northeast of the Areopagus, or "the hill of Ares," lies the Acropolis. In November of 1981, behind a few fallen columns just south of the Parthenon, I tried to speak in tongues myself. I was twenty-one. I was wearing bright blue jeans, a blue T-shirt, and blue canvas Top-Siders. My hair had been clipped short with a pair of travel scissors that folded up and fit in my change pocket.

It was nearly sunset. The guards were herding tourists away from the Parthenon toward the path that led down to the city. I wandered off behind some unpopular ruins to take in the view.

Suddenly, I realized I was all alone. Nobody could see me. I was on top of the Acropolis. I was Greek. And so I tried it out.

There was a slightly justifiable reason for this. Only the day before, at the American Express office in Kolonaki Square, I'd gotten into a discussion with the woman ahead of me in line. I hadn't noticed her until after she'd cashed her traveler's checks, when, as if in return for her drachmas, she'd slipped a pamphlet through the teller's window and bent down to announce into the coin tray, "Jesus is coming." By the expression on the teller's face it didn't appear he was terribly interested in this news. The next thing I knew, the woman had turned around and was looking up at me. She had a scarf covering her head (in compliance with 1 Corinthians 11:5) and a plain, stark, scoured face. She was smiling like crazy and looking deeply and insistently into my eyes as only a religious pamphleteer in a public space can do. And, this time, she'd picked the right guy. At twenty-one years of age, I observed the Areopagite custom of giving anyone a hearing: sidewalk preachers, Krishna devotees, misty Theosophists, angel-crazed Swedenborgians, even, once, a discalced Vietnam vet spouting a mixture of Nietzsche and Zoroastrianism. My position was: What if the nuts are right? It didn't seem impossible that the Truth might come from people the people I knew ridiculed. That day in the Am Ex office, the pamphleteer spoke to me (in pure Pauline fashion, and only a few miles from the original stump) about the Holy Spirit. It was her view that the tingling, Pentecostal experience that the first apostles had felt was available to us today with no diminishment in intensity or alteration in effect. She claimed to have spoken in tongues herself. Even better, she claimed that I could, too. She gave specific instructions. She told me that you had to open your mouth and push out your tongue and "ask for the gift of tongues." She showed me how. I can still picture her face lit by the fluorescent panels overhead, her eyes squeezed shut, her mouth open to offer her plump tongue to God, while I stood looking on, open-minded and embarrassed at once.

Despite the sunbaked Germans departing in tight shorts and crushable hats, the Acropolis managed to seem, as I knelt in the dust that day, sacred. The setting sun sent beams of light across the sea, through Athenian smog, to strike the caryatids rising behind me. Despite my skepticism (which remained all the while), the air and light worked on me as they have on others in that place for millennia. I was three months into an eight-month trip around the world. Everyone I knew was far away. The anonymity of travel had given me the sense that great changes might happen to me. It seemed a terrible loss to miss out on the miraculous just because I didn't believe in it.

Go ahead, I told myself. Try it. No one's looking.

V

The temple to the Unknown God was an insurance policy. It arose from the same motive as fine print or carpet bombing. It covered the Athenians' asses, making sure they didn't forget any god in their sacrifices. Paul, however, stumbling upon the temple, saw not a shrewd policy of universal coverage but something quite different: a gap, an emptiness. Also, for a proselytizer like him, a perfect opening. The Unknown God, the Unseen God, the god who quite literally could not be idolized, was the god he had come to proclaim. "God that made the world, and all things therein, seeing that he is Lord of heaven and earth, dwelleth not in temples made by hand," Paul told the Areopagus (17:24). "Neither is he worshipped with men's hands, as though he needed any thing, seeing he giveth all life, and breath to all things. . . . That they should seek the Lord, if haply they might feel after him, and find him, though he be not far from every one of us: For in him we live, and move, and have our being; as certain also of your own poets have said, For we are also his offspring" (17:25–28).

Paul defined this unknown god largely in negative terms. He was everything the Greeks thought he was not. Consequently, Paul's pitch to the Areopagus had no immediate, sensuous appeal. The problem with the Unknown God was that he couldn't be invoked by visual or physical means.

But what Paul delivered instead was something better: he delivered the idea of the *progressiveness of revelation*. After telling the Athenians all the things that God is not ("We ought not to think that the Godhead is like unto gold, or silver, or stone, graven by art and man's device" [17:29]), Paul then makes a claim with startling theological ramifications. "And the times of this ignorance God winked at; but now commandeth all men everywhere to repent" (17:30). Not only is this diplomatic in absolving the Greeks from their past worship of idols, it also hints at the notion that humanity, in attempting to come in contact with God, proceeds by a series of evolutionary steps. Worshiping an idol may be ignorant, but it's a start. Paul comes to Athens to say that the beginners' class is now over. More precisely, he comes to bear witness to the One who ushered in the next stage.

Jesus himself is the true architect of the idea of a progressive revelation. He constantly broke the Jewish law. He worked on the Sabbath, saying: "My Father worketh hitherto, and I work" (John 5:17). He ate unclean food, justifying: "There is nothing from without a man, that entering into him can defile him: but the things that come out of him, those are they that defile the man" (Mark 7:15). Even more plainly, Jesus told the Pharisees, "For laying aside the commandments of God, ye hold the tradition of men" (Mark 7:8), and "[Thus you make] the word of God of none effect through your tradition, which ye have delivered" (Mark 7:13).

V I

Nothing happened. I opened my mouth. I pushed out my tongue. I prayed for the gift of tongues with as much sincerity and suspended disbelief as I could muster. I waited to see if a supernatural power would commandeer my voice into Koine or Aramaic. My knees began to hurt. Then a guard spotted me and started shouting and waving his arms. And so I got up, brushing off my pants, and went back down to the Plaka, where I spent the rest of the night speaking good old English to a reassuringly palpable Australian girl in cutoffs. I didn't tell her that I'd just tried unsuccessfully to speak in tongues. I didn't tell anyone. The experience merely confirmed my skepticism and made me feel foolish.

What I didn't realize then, however, was that my failure to speak in tongues was consistent with everything the New Testament reports about the nature of the Holy Spirit, namely, that the Holy Spirit never does what people expect. Pentecost had nothing to do with a demonstration of God's power. It was, above all, *practical.* Pentecost remains symbolic of the power of the Divine to end clannishness and expand the universal conversation. Neither of which, thrill-seeking up on the Acropolis, was I particularly trying to do.

V I I

Christians have traditionally been irritatingly smug about the New Testament. They see it as more democratic and less vengeful than the Old Testament, or at least less burdened with religious proscription. This attitude, however, suffers from the placing of a period in the middle of history's ongoing sentence. For if, from an admittedly patronizing Christian viewpoint, the Jewish Law can be streamlined and Greek polytheism superseded, why can't Christianity itself, bound in tradition, be reconsidered and reapplied? The question is: when did revelation stop? Or, put another way: does revelation stop? Paul's words in Acts 17 suggest that it does not, that revelation is ongoing. What "ignorance" are we living in today that God might just now finally be getting sick and tired of? Belief in an Unknown God means that you can never be sure that what you're doing is right, or that what you believe is accurate. Belief in an Unknown God calls for constant reexamination. This makes the whole thing a lot scarier and open to abuse, which is why people generally like to keep things simpler, more tidy, more literal.

But these things are important to keep in mind: that the apostles were constantly amazed at what the Holy Spirit did; that the Holy Spirit went where it wanted to, into the unclean people it wanted to; and that the nature of the Holy Spirit is progressive, inclusive, emancipating, and demanding in ways we cannot foresee.

The Rock

Joseph Caldwell

S I M O N is not an inappropriate name for an apostle. It's a form of Simeon, and Simeon, in Hebrew, means "hearing." Consistent with Hebrew custom, this could be expanded to "one who hears God," or, if preferred, "one whom God has heard." What more could be asked of a follower? Jesus could very aptly — to paraphrase — have said: "Thou art Simon; and through this ear my words will come to my church; and the gates of hell shall not prevail against it."

But Jesus decided an entirely new name — unrecorded among Jews and gentiles — was necessary. Simon, the Ear, became Peter, the Rock. According to Matthew's account, the name was first spoken near Caesarea Philippi. Jesus had asked his disciples:

> Whom do men say that I, the Son of man, am? And they said, Some say that thou art John the Baptist; some Elias; some Jeremias, or one of the prophets. He saith unto them, But whom say ye that I am? And Simon Peter answered and said, Thou art the Christ, the Son of the living God. And Jesus answered and said unto him, Blessed art thou, Simon Bar-jona: for flesh and blood hath not revealed it unto thee, but my Father which is in heaven. And I say also

unto thee, That thou art Peter; and upon this rock I will build my church; and the gates of hell shall not prevail against it.

And so Simon was declared Rock. He was recognized and accepted by Jesus as someone exceptional — even among the twelve he had already chosen. This could have been because Simon, now Peter, had been the first to recognize Jesus as "the Son of the living God," the first to see and to acknowledge his divinity. He, among the twelve, was first in the faith, first in the belief that has sustained Christianity for its two millennia. Jesus had asked a question, and only Simon came up with the right answer — and he was awarded the prize. It was as simple as that.

Or not as simple as that. During the quiz there had been, if not out-and-out cheating, at least some rather insistent prompting. "Flesh and blood hath not revealed it unto thee, but my Father which is in heaven." Simon had been *slipped* the answer. He had been given a singular grace withheld from the others. It was through no merit of his own that he passed the test. Grace, after all, is a gift freely given, unearned and undeserved. The Father, not Jesus, had, in effect, made the selection.

But the Father had not declared him Peter, had not called him Rock, had not said, "Upon this rock I will build my church." Jesus had. Was this merely an extension of the Father's choice? Jesus was, by his own repeated admission, determined to do his Father's will, no matter what it might be. (Two obvious examples come from Luke: "Thy will be done, as in heaven, so in earth," and, at that most anguished moment on the mount of Olives, "Not my will, but thine, be done.") If the Father wanted Simon, then Simon it was.

My guess is that by the time Jesus said "Rock," he was acting on his own. He was going beyond his Father's gift of knowledge and of faith. He was declaring the ramifications of the gift. He was stating the obligations implicit in the election. He was putting a job, a burden, very specifically on Simon. On Peter. This was Jesus' own choice. "And I," not the Father, "say . . . unto thee, That thou art Peter." He must have seen in Simon characteristics — and character — that qualified him for the task being given: to build his church.

And what was meant by "church"? Roman Catholic? Orthodox Greek or Russian? Lutheran, Muslim, Mormon? Obviously not. The church is the people of God. It is the community, it is the sisterhood and brotherhood of the entire human family, the community that Jesus himself was in the process of creating through his Incarnation, his Crucifixion, his Resurrection, and his Ascension. Jesus, through these acts, would create the church, the community. But Peter must fulfill it. And that fulfillment would be the church. Everyone would be qualified because everyone shared the human nature of the Word made flesh. Everyone would be invited because everyone was heir to the redemption; everyone was equally and infinitely loved — no exceptions. The sisterhood and brotherhood — the community — the unity of all humankind, was being established, inseparable and indivisible, and Peter must proclaim it and make it happen. Not, as history has proved, an easy task. And yet, was he not Rock? Was he not Peter?

Well, yes, if Jesus said so. But what had Jesus seen in Simon that inspired him to "build" upon his Father's choice? He must have seen *something*.

Matthew gives no account of Peter's reaction to his commission, but in the same chapter, in the verses immediately following, Jesus tells his apostles that he "must go unto Jerusalem, and suffer many things of the elders and chief priests and scribes, and be killed, and be raised again the third day. Then Peter took him, and began to rebuke him, saying, Be it far from thee, Lord: this shall not be unto thee: But he turned, and said unto Peter, Get thee behind me, Satan: thou art an offence unto me: for thou savourest not the things that be of God, but those that be of men."

In Peter's defense, it should be noted that he had yet to experience the coming of the Holy Spirit and should therefore be allowed a few mistakes and misreadings. Still, his elevation, his anointing — whatever it might be called — seemed to have had little effect on his understanding or his behavior.

Everyone remembers the beginning of Simon's apostolate. As Matthew tells it, "And Jesus, walking by the sea of Galilee, saw two brethren, Simon called Peter, and Andrew his brother, casting a net into the sea: for they were fishers. And he saith unto them, Follow me, and I will make you fishers of men. And they straightway left their nets, and followed him." And yet, in the next episode involving Simon — in both Mark and Matthew — Jesus does not seem to have been very much informed as to Simon's general competence. He and Jesus go to Simon's house. Simon's mother-in-law is sick. Jesus cures the ailing woman. In Mark: "And she ministered unto them"; in Matthew: "And she arose and ministered unto them." The cure was, no doubt, an act of mercy as well as a favor for a friend. And yet there is another element that lurks as a distinct possibility: the future Rock, it would seem, couldn't even fix lunch.

Then there's the incident of the storm at sea. Matthew tells us:

> But the ship was now in the midst of the sea, tossed with waves: for the wind was contrary. And in the fourth watch of the night Jesus went unto them, walking on the sea. And when the disciples

saw him walking on the sea, they were troubled, saying, It is a spirit; and they cried out for fear. But straightway, Jesus spake unto them, saying, Be of good cheer; it is I; be not afraid. And Peter answered him and said, Lord, if it be thou, bid me come unto thee on the water. And he said, Come. And when Peter was come down out of the ship, he walked on the water, to go to Jesus. But when he saw the wind boisterous, he was afraid; and beginning to sink, he cried, saying, Lord, save me! And immediately Jesus stretched forth his hand and caught him, and said unto him, O thou of little faith, wherefore didst thou doubt?

Jesus, of course, is a bit unfair. Peter, eager for his Lord, got out of the boat and began walking toward him *on the water,* a feat (no pun intended) not commonly attempted by the human species. Impulsive he was and of unthinking, unreflecting faith. Buffeted, his faith faltered. But even with his diminished belief, he had enough in reserve to plead for Jesus' help. "Lord, save me!" — the eternal cry of the lost, the vanquished, the abandoned, the plea of those newly aware of the unknowable depths into which they have plunged. Peter didn't sink; he was saved. He may have been rebuked, but the incident was not without triumph. He had experienced a desperate need for help and hadn't hesitated to ask for it. Compared to that, what giddy success would he have achieved if he *had* continued his walk? "Look! I made it! Yippee!" Rock he was, sinkable, and he knew it.

There's another boat scene, much later on, after Jesus' resurrection, and Peter is still very much himself. In John's account, some of the apostles are out fishing again. The risen Jesus appears on the shore, unrecognized. He tells the fishermen to cast their nets over the starboard side, which they do. They are given more fish than they can haul in, and it's then that the "disciple whom

Jesus loved" (John, too modest to name himself in his own Gospel) "saith unto Peter, It is the Lord. Now when Simon Peter heard that it was the Lord, he girt his fisher's coat unto him (for he was naked,) and did cast himself into the sea." They were a hundred yards from land.

Again he is the eager Peter of before, but this time he seems content to swim rather than hazard a walk on the water. Yet the telling detail is that with a hundred yards of swimming ahead of him, he put *on* his clothes. Respect for the Lord? Modesty? An unwillingness to leave his clothes with his colleagues for fear they might be appropriated? Who knows. Still, how many people, before a swim, already stripped, get dressed before jumping into the water? I know of only one. Peter. The Rock.

And none of the disciples seems to have exasperated Jesus more. When the apostles at the Passover supper were having their feet washed by Jesus, it was Peter who said, "Thou shalt never wash my feet. Jesus answered him, If I wash thee not, thou has not part with me." Only then does Peter, still without understanding, allow his feet to be washed, a foretelling of the lowly service to which, as Rock, he is being called.

John ends his entire Gospel account with a dialogue between Jesus and Peter about Peter's fate and the fate of John himself. Of Peter, Jesus says, "When thou shall be old, thou shalt stretch forth thy hands, and another shall gird thee, and carry thee whither thou wouldest not. This spake he, signifying by what death he should glorify God." Without remarking on this prophecy of his martyrdom, Peter asks Jesus about John, and the answer is: "If I will that he tarry till I come, what is that to thee? Follow thou me." And so John ends his Gospel with Jesus again admonishing his Rock, telling him to mind his own business and get on with his ministry.

In fairness to Peter, it should be noted that even before Pentecost and the descent of the Holy Spirit, he had more than a few better moments, most of them obviously unrecorded. That he was privileged, even among the selected twelve, is evidenced by Jesus' invitation to him and to James and John to witness the raising of the daughter of the "ruler of the synagogue's house." An intimacy between Peter and Jesus is being established, an eagerness on the part of the Savior to make Peter more powerfully aware of his compassion and his love.

Yet even here, Peter is unequal to the privilege granted. "And all wept, and bewailed her: but he said, Weep not; she is not dead, but sleepeth. And they laughed him to scorn, knowing that she was dead. And he put them all out, and took her by the hand, and called, saying, Maid, arise."

Difficult as it may be to think of Peter (and James and John) laughing their Master to scorn, there it is, set down by Luke. He, Peter, had been called as witness — and he blew it. He was invited in, and he got himself tossed out.

Also, according to Luke, when Peter was taken by Jesus, again along with James and John, to the top of the mountain for the Transfiguration and the dialogue with Moses and Elias, he, Peter, had a somewhat typical response. "And as he [Jesus] prayed, the fashion of his countenance was altered, and his raiment was white and glistering. And, behold, there talked with him two men, which were Moses and Elias: Who appeared in glory, and spake of his decease which he should accomplish at Jerusalem. But Peter and they that were with him were heavy with sleep." The great salvific act, the death of Jesus, is being discussed — and with no less personages than Moses and Elias. But Peter falls asleep.

And not for the last time. Jesus is in the garden, his final agony already begun. "And he cometh, and findeth them sleeping, and saith unto Peter, Simon, sleepest thou? couldest not thou watch one hour?" Twice more Jesus would return and on the third return would simply say, "Sleep on now, and take your rest: it is enough, the hour is come."

While this may sound as if Jesus had finally reconciled himself to Peter's insufficiencies, he will, not long after, be given further cause for exasperation. In John's account, after Jesus has surrendered himself to his captors, "Simon Peter, having a sword, drew it, and smote the high priest's servant, and cut off his right ear. The servant's name was Malchus. Then said Jesus unto Peter, Put up thy sword into the sheath: the cup which my Father hath given me, shall I not drink it?"

This weary admonition, mournful, resigned, would be the last that Jesus would speak to his chosen Rock before his crucifixion, but before the night had passed, Peter would give cause for a rebuke so mournful that words would become unnecessary.

Earlier that evening, at the Passover meal (in Matthew's account), Jesus had said:

> All ye shall be offended because of me this night: for it is written, I will smite the shepherd, and the sheep of the flock shall be scattered abroad. But after I am risen again, I will go before you into Galilee. Peter answered and said unto him, Though all men shall be offended because of thee, yet will I never be offended. Jesus said unto him, Verily I say unto thee, That this night, before the cock crow, thou shalt deny me thrice. Peter said unto him, Though I should die with thee, yet will I not deny thee.

Later that night, after his sleep, after his rash act with the sword:

Peter sat without in the palace: and a damsel came unto him, saying, Thou also wast with Jesus of Galilee. But he denied before them all, saying, I know not what thou sayest. And when he was gone out into the porch, another maid saw him, and said unto them that were there, This fellow was also with Jesus of Nazareth. And again he denied with an oath, I do not know the man. And after a while came unto him they that stood by, and said to Peter, Surely thou also art one of them; for thy speech bewrayeth thee. Then began he to curse and to swear, saying, I know not the man. And immediately the cock crew.

Jesus, of course, was a fool. Who but a fool would knowingly take simple Simon and proclaim him the Rock? Who but a fool would entrust the future of his church to an impulsive, unthinking perjurer? Who but a fool would become human; who but a fool would take on the flesh and, in the flesh, accept ignominy, humiliation, abandonment, and death if it was in his power to escape? Only a fool would define his church as the entire human community, bound by love for him and for one another — and then compound that foolishness by presuming that he could transform flesh, ignorant, violent, perjuring flesh, into the Rock upon which that community would be built. Only Jesus, the fool, would do it.

But Jesus, of course, was not a fool. He knew exactly what he was doing. His Rock was not a compression of minerals. It was not stone. It was the human clay from which all are fashioned. It was, it is, the flesh. The flesh is the Rock. Flesh and faith. It was in the flesh that Jesus was born; it was in the flesh that he suffered and died; it was in the flesh that he rose from the grave; it was in the flesh that he ascended, retaining his human nature forever. And it is with and through the flesh — erring, exasperating human flesh

143

in which dwells a stumbling faith, the Rock made of mortal clay — that his work is to be accomplished. All flesh is rock.

Saint Paul, in his lengthy letter to the Romans, says, "They that are in the flesh cannot please God. But ye are not in the flesh, but in the Spirit. . . ." Paul, when he wrote those words, was, we are led to believe, filled with the Holy Spirit. Be that as it may, he was also full of beans.

Snake Bite

Ann Patchett

And these signs shall follow them that believe: In my name shall they cast out devils; they shall speak with new tongues; they shall take up serpents; and if they drink of any deadly thing, it shall not hurt them; they shall lay hands on the sick, and they shall recover.

MARK 16:17–18

THE churches that I pass as I drive through town, the many, many churches in the South that I do not belong to, I know mostly for their architecture. I may have the vaguest understanding of their doctrine, possibly I knew someone once who was a member, but the thing that draws people to that particular building is almost always unknown to me, and this seems right. They are not my churches, and most of what happens in any church remains between the parishioners themselves or between the parishioners and God. In our faith, as in our personal lives, other people are only given access to any real information about our beliefs when something has gone wrong. I have never attended service at the Church of the Holiness Faith. I have rarely seen their buildings, but things in that church go wrong often enough that most people in the South know why this congregation gathers and how they pray.

There are basically two reasons why the Church of the Holiness Faith turns up in the newspapers: either a member has been bitten by a snake, or the state is trying to close the church down because someone has been bitten. If a member has been bitten, he or she will probably need to die before the story surfaces. Those who are merely sick tend to lie low, wait out the swelling, the fevers and terrible pain at home. Sometimes the refusal to go to the hospital will make the local news. The members of their church pray for the recovery of their sick. If the bitten member does not recover, a court case usually ensues. Southern states have wrestled for generations as to whether or not it is legal for a man or a woman to pick up a snake as a testament of faith. Occasionally, a minister is charged with some degree of murder. While the investigations drag on, the congregation scatters. They meet at the homes of the faithful to pray. They continue to pick up snakes, or not pick up snakes, as the spirit moves them.

In this way they are direct descendants of their forefather, George Hensley of Grasshopper Valley, Tennessee. The legend goes that in the early 1900s, Hensley, who read the Bible with a passionate heart and a literal mind, became so overwhelmed by the eighteenth verse of the sixteenth chapter of Mark that he ran into the mountains and grabbed up the first rattlesnake he could find. Having survived the encounter unharmed, he went into the valley to become the prophet of a new religion. Since then, groups of people in the Appalachia region of the South have been handling snakes because they claim the Bible tells them to. The snakes are kept in wooden boxes near the pulpit. There is a sermon, music is played, members begin to move around, to dance, to speak in tongues. Some nights several people will reach into the boxes and take out a snake or two, other nights the snakes are

146

left alone. They only do this when they are so moved by the Holy Spirit, and when it happens that a snake bites, it is because for a second, a second that passes so quickly they themselves might not be able to recognize it, their faith has wavered.

In the Gospel According to Saint Mark, Jesus was crucified for saying that he would tear the temple down and rebuild it in three days. His metaphor, that he himself was the temple of God, was misunderstood by the people and taken as a threat against a building. The literalists put him to death.

Jesus foresaw their misunderstanding. In Mark, he relied heavily on parables to spread his teaching. In chapter 4, the disciples asked Jesus about this method. "And he said unto them, Unto you it is given to know the mystery of the kingdom of God; but unto them that are without, all these things are done in parables: That seeing they may see, and not perceive; and hearing they may hear, and not understand; lest at any time they should be converted, and their sins should be forgiven them." The people who were as yet unsaved were never meant to understand. They had not yet been given access to metaphor. They could hear the story of how the farmer's seed fell both in thistles and on fertile ground, but they could not understand that Jesus spoke figuratively about the souls of men. It was their role to follow the prophecies, to put the Son of God to death. And yet it was after his death and resurrection, as he was reunited with the doubting disciples, that Jesus spoke of handling the serpent. Weren't those disciples (the only ones who saw the true meaning of the parables at the time) meant to understand this as a symbol, the completion of the cycle begun with a snake in the garden of Eden? Now we can handle temptation, take evil into our hands and overcome it. Or maybe the newly risen Christ was telling them that those

147

who believe would know everlasting life. The snake can take the body but not the soul. Or possibly, Jesus was speaking to George Hensley. Maybe what he was saying was "Go into your yard and pick up a snake, and if your heart is pure and open to me, it just won't bite you."

"I handle serpents whenever I get anointed by the Lord," Liston Pack told his local Tennessee newspaper in 1973. Pack was the minister at the Holiness Church of God in Jesus' Name. He fought in the courts for the right to handle his snakes, saying that his congregation believed in the literal correctness of every word in the Bible, from Genesis to Revelation. But why did he choose to follow the sixteenth chapter of Mark? Why not Mark 11:23? "For verily I say unto you, That whosoever shall say unto this mountain, Be thou removed, and be thou cast into the sea; and shall not doubt in his heart, but shall believe that those things which he saith shall come to pass; he shall have whatsoever he saith." If the Bible could withstand a completely literal interpretation, wouldn't there be a sect of people standing purposefully in front of a mountain?

Tennessee is often referred to as "the buckle on the Bible Belt." Last year the state senate tried to pass a bill that would require the posting of the Ten Commandments in all public buildings. Another bill being debated would require evolution to be taught as a theory along with creationism, reminding us all that Tennessee was that state that hosted the Scopes "monkey trial." If the religious climate was not enough to engender the Church of the Holiness Faith, then the ample supply of poisonous snakes might be. The region has rattlesnakes, cottonmouths, and copperheads. There are more than enough snakes to fill every wooden box in every church of the Holiness Faith. Snakes are easily found in rocky areas, beneath fallen trees, or on the road at night just as the sun goes down. They are dangerous, but the odds are not so severely stacked against the handlers as one might think. Adult pit vipers control the amount of venom released in a strike based on their assessment of danger. They are less likely to strike if they have been recently fed. They are more likely to strike in the autumn, when their vision is impaired by the molting of their skin. Most fatalities from snake bites occur in the very young and the very old, and with every snake bite survived, a person's blood develops antibodies to venom. There are members of the church who have been bitten over a hundred times. They are themselves the antidote to the poison. At one point there was a church in possession of an Indian cobra. "That cobra is just like handling a red worm if you get anointed with the spirit," Liston Pack told reporters. The snake was handled without incident, which was fortunate, as a cobra bite is much more likely to be fatal than the bite of any North American snake. Also fatal, but much less rare than snakes in usage, is the "salvation cocktail," a mixture of strychnine and fruit juice. When members hold blow torches to their skin, the skin does burn. There are some testaments of faith the body cannot overcome.

"And he sighed deeply in his spirit, and saith, Why doth this generation seek after a sign? verily I say unto you, There shall no sign be given unto this generation" (Mark 8:12).

Perhaps the Church of the Holiness Faith tests the Lord thy God, or perhaps they only seek a more visceral connection to his suffering. As a Catholic, I am always looking at crucifixes. In many churches Jesus' legs are lean but well muscled. The hole in his side is a bare slit. His head is tilted, and the pain on his face is the pain of disappointment, sorrow rather than agony. In many affluent churches, the body of Christ has vanished altogether. The wood of the cross is clean and smooth. Its well-lit planes have become art. I once attended a Mass where all four sides of the cross were of equal length, making a plus sign, a positive message for happy people. But go into the Catholic churches in the poorest parts of New Mexico, Los Angeles, New York. Jesus is dying on the cross for your sins, and the death is excruciating. The tendons on the neck strain. The mouth opens to scream. The body is thin from starvation, every rib a tragedy. The blood is bright red to impress upon the parish its freshness. It isn't dabbed at the hands. This blood streams and coats the skin from the five holes and every thorn in the biting crown.

For us to love Christ, he must suffer more than we do, and when it seems he's suffered less, we turn away. In parts of the South, suffering is as plentiful as snakes. The suffering and hardships that have befallen the areas in and around the Appalachian Mountains are often beyond a person's control. But Jesus reached toward the violence that came for him. He did not spare himself his cross, but picked it up for the good of us all. What if this is the moment in Christ's life we choose to emulate? To be with him not in the stillness of prayer but in the storm of his death? What could be more powerful than to, for a moment, control that over which there is no control, to handle at the same time the literal snake and the metaphorical devil? The chances that the snake will be returned to its box without incident are better than the five empty chambers in Russian roulette, and for that moment of chance you will have followed the word of God in its most literal interpretation.

In the South, there is something righteous about using the word "literal" when speaking about how to read the Bible. It tends to be equated with "true," as if to say, I am reading the Bible the hard way. And if, in fact, reading the Bible literally means picking up snakes, then I will admit that it is a strenuous way to read. To interpret the Bible, to read it for the meaning that can be found through exploring its metaphors, is often seen as soft, the practice of those who are looking to reinforce their own beliefs or justify their actions. But the use of metaphor in how we reason and communicate is a sure sign of our intellectual growth and development. I can only hope that looking for God in the deeper meanings of the Bible is a sure sign of our spiritual growth. If I woke up tomorrow and believed that picking up a snake was what God wanted of me, would I pick one up? If it was true that the snake wouldn't strike as long as my faith did not waver, would the snake strike?

Corpus Christi

Eurydice

"TAKE and eat, this is my body, which is given for you." This unnerving call to the Eucharist has been invoked for two thousand years now, hundreds of thousands of times a day across the globe. Its primal, cannibalistic holy words help assure the partakers' fertility and potential immortality through the enactment of this most important feast: the eating of our God, of our sacrificial "slain lamb," of the transubstantiated bread and wine that is in some primeval and unsymbolic way the thirty-three-year-old crucified and risen Jesus in flesh and blood.

As Saint Thomas observes, Christ didn't say "This bread is my body," he said "This is my body" — which indicates that "this" is bread no longer. Each eucharistic bread loaf *is* Christ's *Passion,* Christ's body dispersed among the open mouths of the faithful, an edible manifestation of that very body he gave up for the sake of the perennially hungry believer.

"Take this . . . and drink from it: this is the cup of my blood." The awesome double consecration of bread and wine (which are Christ in his terrible death, in the separation of blood from his body) engages our natural senses, providing us with a *physical* knowledge of God. It brings us together and transports us outside our socioeconomic and utilitarian roles and into the rare opportunity to share sensual and spiritual pleasure, to be a society.

Wine drinking (even more than the brutal springtime sacrifice of a young male god) has been the focal point of sacred blessings, festivals, libations, and iconographies from the earliest human civilizations to this day. Osiris and Hathor, Dionysus and Bacchus, Elijah and Noah, were patrons of wine; Shinto, Hindu, Chinese, and Jewish ceremonies employ it, and even the Qur'an associates it with the grace of God. The turning of water to wine was Christ's first public miracle, and his final official act was the naming of his last cup of wine as his new covenant and urging his gathered disciples to keep on drinking it in remembrance of his passage. Not surprisingly, altar wines escaped Prohibition.

The phenomenon of the sacred meal is one of those religious universals that know no boundaries, whether cultural or temporal. Mankind has consistently acknowledged the mysterious character of eating and drinking — as an essential communion with the cosmos and the unspeakable (i.e., God) — and has regularly attached a cultic aspect to it. These age-old rituals reconfirm our deep pagan bond to the physical world, reminding us that we emerge from nature and return to it, and for the short time when we remain a tangible part of nature, we sustain our life by taking what it offers and assimilating it into our selves.

By swallowing the Eucharist, we become *united* with Christ via the mediation of material elements and are thus able to be resurrected *with* him. The idea is that Christ's suffering saves *us* from suffering, and from having to sacrifice ourselves: "Whoever eats my flesh and drinks my blood has eternal life, and I will raise him up" (John 6:54). Christ's physical death magically brings physical ease, happiness, and deliverance for the rest of us.

The Eucharist is the most sensual of the sacraments: it establishes sacramentality in consuming and evokes in the celebrant the intimacy of the Last Supper. Its vocabulary is revealing: eat me, be faithful, drink my blood, raise you up, celebrate. Here is Jesus Christ making love to us. In the devotion, inside his bride (the church), the Logos is *incarnate,* a Real Presence, penetrating and all-consuming even as he is being forever consumed.

AS a child, I went through many profound reactions to my weekly Communion: at first I felt sheer indiscriminate gratification at a time when any oral stimulation was inordinately welcome. That was followed by a giddy sensual joy — because the alcohol was aged and sweet and gave me a light head; the bread was soft and sweet and preciously rationed, unlike any other bread; the feeding spoon was miniature and made of gold; the server was sheathed in red and gold gowns; and my family embraced me enthusiastically as soon as I gulped it down. Next came my sense of awe at swallowing this Communion: I feared my hubris, I wasn't big enough to contain a godly morsel, to retransmogrify it into spirit and soul, to not shit it out but forever after hold it within my mortal being. I spent my Sundays tracing the course of that tiny burning bite down my esophagus through inner niche and cranny, intestines small and large, obsessively anxious to avoid the inevitable blasphemy of peeing out my own God. But my dumb little body always embarrassed me.

In time, inconsistencies I couldn't forgive, contradictions that left me near insane, began to torment me. I had trouble mentally processing the logic-crashing paradox that was condensed in that spoonful of crumb and wine. I understood by then the use of simile and metaphor and could have grasped the *symbolism* of the weekly rite and moved on, if my grandfather, who was our priest, had not insisted that this was *not* a metaphor; I wasn't asked to *imagine,* he said, that the wine from the cedar barrel in our musty cellar became Christ's blood after he blessed it and raised the chalice. It *was* blood. As my grandfather had never gone swimming or singing at taverns or fishing or dancing or even sightseeing; and fasted twice a week and built churches, monasteries, and museums; and all day intoned Byzantine psalms to himself, his self-denial automatically made him an authority in matters of faith. I couldn't argue with him. It was then that I also began to feel hypochondriac about the tiny ornate spoon I had once admired, and as I waited in the long line of communicants I worried about the germs in the ad hoc mouths that licked it off before my turn could come.

I knew the priest lent his voice and his hand to Christ — not as an actor but a humble incarnation in the service of the people who assembled around the altar as the apostles had around the dinner table — as he said: "Take this, all of you, and eat it." But having lost the ability to believe in any direct incarnation, I was left, at prepubescence, face-to-face with the bottom-line ugly reality of it: the barbarism. So I quit going to church, and the Homeric fights that ensued week after week between my relatives and me propped up their stern sense of honor against my logic, God against me, my tradition against my education, and tore apart our family fabric until I had no anchor and decided to run away from home. That was how I came to America at the age of fifteen. I did not receive Communion again for years.

Fifteen years later, I have come full circle: now I savor that tiny aromatic drop of body-and-blood, the tangy, warm wine-and-crumb that connects me to all I come from, my island, my dead granddad, my living tongue, my fertility, my euphoria, my body, and, I dare use the word, my soul. And I have come to understand the importance of rituals.

My ancestral Coptic-Orthodox Church celebrates an openly pagan Christianity that is born of our awe of the same hurricanes and earthquakes and accidents that have timelessly haunted humanity. It gives people hope to go on when all seems futile, when death is at the end of every effort. Its local Marys carry on the epithets and attributes of extinct indigenous nymphs. In my maternal village, for instance, our priest sacrificed a muscular, flower-garlanded bull to Christ on a certain saint's day; after he had toured the village streets to a merry accompaniment of singing, lyre playing, and praying all the way to the church courtyard, the bull was briskly decapitated, adroitly skinned, and cut into bits that women cooked in large pots on log fires and served to the congregation after Mass. The recipe was unique to that saint's day, but the feast resembled dozens in the Christian calendar commemorating the martyrdom of local saints on different dates in each village. These feasts marked the social life of the community, bound the people to each other and to their culture, and afforded free food for the poor and days of civic equality and class interaction that were unprecedented. Christ upheld our democratic customs. Even more than magical reassurance, *this* has been the primary function of religion from the beginning of time: communal sensual partaking.

THIS is why it makes no sense that the official Christian Church is under the illusion that it needs to rob us of our senses in order to keep us under control. When the church calls itself "the body of Christ," it refers to a body that is desexualized, flagellated, shaming. And though the Gospels give much more attention to the miracles, parables, aphorisms, symbolic acts, and human relations of Jesus than to his final martyrdom, with the passage of time his church has gorily capitalized on the "masochism" of his crucifixion and has consistently used it to hold us in fear of sexuality and in thrall of all suffering.

We know Jesus considered the spirit to be inextricably involved with the body. He taught everything *on* the body, his own and others'. He healed, whipped, and resurrected human flesh. He understood the pain, pleasure, and pressure our bodies feel. That was his gift: physical compassion. He broke the Jewish Levitical taboos of cleanness and uncleanness, and provocatively ignored the intricate laws of purity of his day's official sexist faith, which regulated all dealings with the dead, food, and gender. He touched the lepers, the blind, the dead, the whores, and the bleeding women — all the forbidden castes. So it is still shocking how soon after his deification the old body-restraining, intimacy-regulating taboos he had abhorred were reinstated by his own church, often fiercer than they had been before.

As Jesus the iconoclast was turned into Jesus the icon, his vision was castrated and his social criticism defanged. Even the most cursory history of Christianity reveals the irrelevancy of our sexual repression to both Christ and his vision of heaven on earth.

In its beginning, the Jesus movement arose as a freedom-loving and eros-evoking reform, drawing strength from communal agape. As it grew in numbers, the emperors recognized its usefulness in placating unsatisfied masses, and professional church fathers, who fanaticized and at the same time legitimized it, took it over. By the time Christianity became Constantine's official imperial faith, replacing the worship of the emperor himself, its power was so substantial it had to be controlled, manipulated, and "normalized" by the ruling bureaucracy. This task was undertaken by both practical and philosophical means.

A. The gradual establishment of the monarchic bishop system and the three-tiered structure of the presbyteriate was the church's first major deviation from Christ's radically egalitarian teachings. (Its timid precursor had been the Christian elder-presbyter system in Jerusalem, which had absorbed the Judaic priestly caste.) The establishment of a permanently hired priesthood endowed with disciplinary powers over the laity inaugurated the serialization and massification of the laity, which until then had stayed fused, and the growing desecularization of education that reinforced the laity's oppression. As knowledge came under theocratic control, the original trend that had pulled the upper classes and intellectuals to Christ's church was reversed: the laity was now educated by its priests, and intellectuals had to become either monks or heretics.

The second step in this autocratic progression was the declaration of the primacy of the Roman bishop, who eventually replaced the collective leadership of the bishops as the supreme head of the church, absorbing the imperial trappings and arrogant pomp of Roman rule into the praxis of the church. In the following centuries, the Roman bishop had the singular power to exempt himself from his own moral rulings. Dozens of popes fathered illegitimate children and were often succeeded by their sons, like the emperors of old.

The Sermon on the Mount had made clear what Jesus thought of such hierarchical structures. To meet its governing needs, the church transposed Christ's vision of a nonauthoritarian, translucent society out of the world and onto the promised society of heaven, which ironically *justified* suffering in this world. Christians ended up living for the rewards of heaven. And entry to that intangible, egalitarian afterlife was restricted, kept tightly in the hands of the hierarchy, which bartered it at will and for profit. Thus Christendom's heaven replaced life on earth.

The third step toward the Christian church's unprecedented iron rule of theocracy was the obligatory celibacy of the all-male clergy, enforced in the eleventh century during the Gregorian reforms. This process completely reversed Christ's vision that all the members of his church were also members of the priesthood. Perpetual priestly celibacy served to solidify geopolitical power and prestige in the hands of the pope and to set apart his powerless representatives as morally superior beings; to prevent second sons of nobles from claiming positions as local bishops without papal consent; and to stop married priests' families from inheriting and selling ecclesiastic offices and properties.

The final step in the structural and spiritual sclerosis of the church was the notion of the infallibility of the pope, proclaimed in 1870 with the stroke of a pope's pen, which in effect turned him into God. The sovereign pope became the only subject in the Catholic church.

Clearly, civic laws are irrelevant to the preservation and dispensation of God's word, which is the clergy's only confirmed task. Secular power is antithetical to Christ's teachings. Yet the pope today remains the ultimate temporal ruler for 60 million Christians who are excluded from *real* religious function and who are a priori inessential members of the church. And after two thousand years of continuous institutionalization, having survived every big revolution intact, the church believes it can endure without change.*

B. After the Hellenistic and before the Byzantine period, Christians had viewed the flesh of Christ as utterly continuous with human flesh. That was the original genius of the Christian faith: in the conception, birth, nurturing, and death of Christ, every human physiological process was reaffirmed. Christ's incarnation expunged the "disorder" introduced into the human body by Adam's fall. The Christian religion initially prevailed primarily because it preached *Every*man/woman's salvation, equality, freedom, brotherhood. It was itself a revolution. That was much more important to most believers than their allegorical victory over death.

But when the Christians were ushered into power by Emperor Constantine (who used Christianity to found his rule and was later sanctified), the church was inevitably co-opted, its message distorted by newer apologists keen to help the powers that be control the masses. Archaic pagan rites were transferred onto Christian customs, saints succeeded old demigods, and the Christian codes of behavior were adapted to ways of life developed long before the advent of Christianity. Roman administration was moved into the bishop's palace. Bishops assumed the duties, tiaras, and ritualized tasks of courtiers and emperors.†

One of the easiest ways to deflate the insurgent democratic ethos of the Christian faith was to switch its emphasis away from

---

* Examples: The Vatican disavowed the responsibility of the Jews for the death of Jesus only in 1993. Threats of excommunication and the casting of priests or nuns out of their orders for insubordination to papal doctrine continue to this day.

† A memorable example: In A.D. 630, three hundred prostitutes demonstrated against the governor of Syracuse; to placate them, he appointed the Catholic bishop of Syracuse as Imperial Inspector of Brothels.

life and toward then-current Gnostic obsession with the democracy of *death*. In synods and encyclicals, bishops placed new emphasis on the Christian worship of the dead, cruelly reminding the flock of its inevitable destination.

As Christianity came under the influence of the dominant Graeco-Roman world view, which espoused the dichotomy between body and soul, it exchanged the totality of the Jesus movement for the fashionable Stoic ethic, which reacted to the self-destructive Roman moral decadence by advocating a sexuality devoid of pleasure and used solely for procreation. Soon enough, Porphyry's old phrase about Plotinus, "Shame at being in the body," somehow came to represent Christian piety. Jesus' political message of across-the-board civic freedom and personal responsibility came to mean "freedom *from* the body."

Rome's vestal virgins, the Essene Jews, the Encratite and Gnostic thinkers, were all practicing abstinence then, preaching in their distinct bleak ways that the end of the "corrupt age" would be brought about by the "boycott of the womb," that sexuality was a token of human bondage, and that sex contributed to the animal cycle of mortality. Doomsday scenarios were so de rigueur that in order to gain philosophical prestige, Christian leaders felt pressure to legitimate their faith by incorporating these pagan forebodings into Christianity.

Monasticism was the first outcome of this influence, popularized by the charismatic Anthony of the Egyptian desert. The less talented sons of large families, or men who could not marry because of money or bad health, or men and women of privileged classes who disdained the forced dislocations of marriage, childbirth, and bereavement found honorable escape in asceticism. A woman's virgin body granted her some freedom from the responsibilities of daily life; her untouched flesh, mirroring the purity of the garden of Eden, afforded her higher public status than she could know within a Roman or Jewish or Christian marriage. At first, monasticism did not massively affect the Christian populace.

At the beginning, the laity simply wanted holy persons it could consult, and it was drawn to the *strangeness* of the ferocious ascetic virgins who lived shorn of normal human attributes and had no fear of death or need for continuity through procreation. Numerous relics of massacred virgins were being preserved in churches and were thought to spread fertility, health, and longevity to the living.* But their spiritual power did not encroach on the profane life of the community and its collective enjoyment of the theater, public baths, and hippodrome at a time when sexual shame was unknown among the upper classes. Those early Christians could not have foreseen how soon and overwhelmingly their own church would come to restrict their private physical pleasures in the name of God.

In Paul's time, the resurrection of the dead was still understood "as taking place through the nature of the human body, and accomplished every day . . . [via] the succession of children born from us" (Polybius, *Vita Thecla* 5). Famously, Paul himself wrote in Galatians that in Christ "there is neither male nor female . . . neither slave nor free" (3:28).† But Christian values began shifting. The misogyny of the Greeks crept its way into the Christian

---

* Ironically, saints specialized in curing problems they would have known nothing about. For example, Saint Thecla, Paul's virgin companion, helped wronged wives with love potions or pregnancy/sterility advice.

† Also: "[Jesus] has broken down the dividing wall of hostility, by abolishing in his flesh the law of commandments and ordinances, that he might create in himself one new man in place of two, so making peace, and might reconcile us both to God in one body" (Eph. 2:16).

exegesis, and Paul cautioned, "It is shameful for a woman to speak in church" (1 Cor. 14:35). Thomas Aquinas went on to define women as misbegotten men. Soon after that, procreation struck younger Christian theologians as a central contradiction to be resolved.

Until Augustine converted in the fourth century, Christians had understood the story of Adam and Eve as a story about responsibility and free will, noting that as Adam and Eve left Paradise, God encouraged them to give names to things and rule the world. Augustine had previously belonged to the Manichaean sect, which believed the earth to be the futile kingdom of the devil and all procreation to be diabolical. The sect asked continence from its members and the use of contraception or abortion from sympathizers. (Augustine felt grave guilt for keeping a long-time mistress and fathering a son with her, then banishing her for a suitable wife, before converting to Christianity.) The Manichaeans saw the sexual instinct not as a merciful gift to Adam from God to help him overcome death but as a demonic possession of the world; they believed that permanent evil, present in all humans, was responsible for the mindless continuation of a degenerate humanity through the act of intercourse and that if sexual activity would cease, the tumultuously repeated constraints of birth and death would be broken. Like other Gnostics, the Manichaeans preached the imminent end of the age.

Anxious to make himself a place in his new faith, Augustine passed these old-fashioned fatalisms into the new Christian society by defining the normal sexual drive as *poena reciproca,* punishment on Adam's descendants for his crime. He preached that sexual pleasure infected the conceived child with original sin — i.e., with eternal damnation. Sex and the grave stood at each end of every human life, delineating the two poles in between which roared a cascade of helpless misery, ignorance, malice, and violence forever after.

This pessimistic vision of life on earth was brusquely adopted by church authorities who found in it a useful justification of the urge to shepherd people by a higher authority — by God's representatives on earth. Carnal sin superseded all other sins, and subsequent theologians went as far as to preach that isolation from sex was the main reason Christ had come to earth.* For the next 1,500 years the church went on to instill the terror of pleasure in its people. And to this day, even those who think of Genesis only as literature, or those who are not Christian, live in a culture indelibly shaped by Augustine's dark reading of a text written down by Hebrew tribes thousands of years ago.

Augustine's theology was predicated on one line from Genesis: "And the eyes of both of them were opened and they knew they were naked." In contrast to other contemporary Greek or Syrian Christian writers, Augustine, the lowly African bishop of Hippo, read there an instant of sexual shame (perhaps due to his own sexual misgivings). In driven prose, Augustine narrowed Christian theology down to the paradigm of the "indecent" *summa voluptas* of orgasm, which escaped conscious control and which marked those limits of the conscious self that had first stunned Adam and Eve. His interpretation of that crucial moment when Adam and Eve made their wills independent from God and felt their bodies alien and uncontrollable presented the popes with reason to warn against the risks of free will. His reading stuck: disobedience was the cause of evil, and sex was its manifestation.

So Augustine's politically expedient belief in the moral impo-

* Example: Clement, *The Stromateis.*

tence of human beings confirmed the need for universal government and helped popes consolidate their power by imposing celibacy or unnatural moral laws on the nations and governments of the world. The church hierarchy realized that if it could dictate the innermost secret desires of kings, presidents, and plebes, its power would remain absolute and unchallengeable. That is why the Christian Church, even in this most bloody of centuries, views humanity's crimes as being committed in married people's bedrooms.* And that is how the seed was laid for the sadomasochistic dominance of the church over our natural instincts, which has resulted in a plethora of neuroses and pathologies. Ever since Augustine, the sexual act has retained a central negative role in our relationship with ourselves and our sense of self-worth; even in our post-Freudian world, we fear the deranging effects of lust and seek our pleasure in dark places, guiltily associating normal bodily desire with an evil and ineffable transgression.

O N E of the most authoritative rebuttals of Augustine in his own time came from a member of the monastic diaspora, John Cassian, who sought to modify the denial of the freedom of will implied in Augustine's notion of predestination. Cassian argued that sexual temptation was universal, thus "natural to man," "congenital" — i.e., "planted by the will of the Lord not to injure us, but to help us." He also thought sexual drive led to compassion.

Augustine's most famous opponent was Julian, bishop of Eclanum, who movingly defended the *calor genitalis* — that dif-

---

* Example: In Nazi Germany, the Catholic Church declared contraception illegal because it limited military manpower. It was a sin to kill unborn children, but an honor to birth cannon fodder.

fused heat of ecstasy that medical opinion then held necessary for reproduction (without it, scientists of the time thought, the race would end). He argued that sexuality was indispensable to our species, having been offered to us by God in his mercy.* Julian contradicted Augustine's credo of despair by maintaining that sexual desire did not *have* to be renounced and was not corrupted. He in fact thought it impious to suggest that the sexual urge was not what God had blessed in Adam and Eve and what priests consecrated during marriage. Julian preached that sex was what free choice made it. Human libido was amenable to the will and blameworthy only in harmful excess; its antisocial uses were banal by-products that could be soothed by the study of the Gospels.

Yet Julian ended up portrayed in history as the heretic and Augustine as the saint. And the laity became sexually subjected to the harsh formative orders of its popes.†

With the passage of time, Christians who disagreed with Augustine's credo were excommunicated, tortured, eradicated. Thousands were burned at the stake, condemned to "shunning" and poverty, sent on far-flung pilgrimages and agonizing penances, forced to confess to heresy and thrown into perpetual imprisonment, all in the name of and for the sake of the God of

---

* Sexual pleasure between a married couple still posed no problems to celibate church fathers like John Chrysostom at the time; Chrysostom wrote of the woman "receiving the man's seed with rich pleasure."

† The current pope's *Familiaris* encyclical suggests married continence as a way to avoid unwanted childbirth and to protect wives from the freebooting mentality of the husbands (by taking the pill, wives unleash their husbands' sex drives and end up helpless in their clutches). The pope sees women as the *victims* of sex. Like a pornographer, the pope defines sex not as an expression of love but as degradation.

Love. Guilt was presumed, suspicion of a crime constituted a crime, properties were confiscated, and the taint of the heretic fell on the accused's family for generations. The *hoc omnus gene* was kept in fear just as in Roman and Pharisaic times.

Also with the passage of time, revivalist sects were born that persisted and found refuge in exile — Anabaptists, Quakers, Jehovah's Witnesses, born-agains — most in the Americas. But there again, the moneymen and strongmen eventually organized the new Christian sects into manageable and profitable institutions. (Latin America espoused a liberation theology, but the resources and prestige of competing Christian churches and the iron rule of the pope diffused it.) It now seems improbable that we may ever return to a pre-Pauline sexual innocence and natural unself-consciousness, even as that sort of quest has become the dominant spiritual quest for many social groups in our society.

NEVERTHELESS, the Incarnation and Resurrection of Jesus are central affirmations of the human body. Christ is the Word made *Flesh*. What would Christ's Passion have been if he hadn't had mortal flesh? His intention was not to deify suffering but to transcend it, to set his life, not his death, as an example. Fighting nature is a product of human vanity, not divine inspiration. The systematic clerical demonization of the flesh is antilife and anti-Christ. Disembodiment is a form of loveless, insecure human atrophy. Clearly, this was not Christ's intention. Christ sent a message not of self-abuse but of self-transformation — of embodiment, of heaven on earth.*

---

* "The end of all God's works is embodiment," wrote the the eighteenth-century theologian Friedrich Oetinger.

I used to wonder as a child what Christ might have looked like, and imagined him as a buff carpenter — a peasant muscleman with thick body hair, a prominent nose, sensual lips — or as a thin, gawky, nearsighted, listless intellectual. I wondered if he'd ever gotten tipsy drinking all that wine, and if he'd had an erection when Mary rubbed his feet with her fragrant hair* or when Judas kissed him on the lips or as he died on the cross. Jesus was the Proteus of my early imagination, a polymorphous immateriality that gave me cause to create. That is why, I think, we have no descriptions of him by the evangelists — so that he could be a *universal* deity. The pellucid, effeminate dying blond male whose pitiable likeness graces millions of churches across this planet has no historical or theological justification.† We worship Christ on the cross as he lies wilted, a helpless, defeated, mournful corpse, because the church fathers once again considered it advantageous to the longevity of their rule. The Christ of the Last Supper is not our central icon, even though it may be more authentic.

We know that the biblical Jesus passionately engaged with

* There are few scenes as sensual in all literature as the ministrations of the whore toward the happily passive, appreciative Jesus. The washing and drying of his feet with her oiled hair evokes affection that is not verbatim reported. It is evident that Mary Magdalene is attracted to Jesus and that Jesus responds to her devotion. She is beloved by him more than any other woman. And she is the apostles' apostle, credited with being the first to witness and announce the Resurrection. But later, his church disencouraged her worship, unable to refurbish the reformed whore Mary as easily as it did the Mary who became the Virgin; as a result the Magdalene cult never rose to its potential height, and her place as Christ's honored intimate and as the harbinger of the most important news of the New Testament remains underexploited.

† The first painting of Jesus came four hundred years after his death, and even then he was not an expiring wuss.

everyone he met. Much like an energetic modern politician on the campaign trail, he appealed to gentiles and tax collectors, housewives and prostitutes, and even reveled in his public adoration. His mere touch raised the underprivileged from the shadows. There was, in the words of theologian Paul Tillich, an "eternal now" about his life. He was fully present to the unknown woman in Bethany who anointed his head and to the street woman who interrupted his dinner in the house of Simon the Pharisee to wash Jesus' feet with her hair (Luke 7:36); and so deeply did he trust in body language that he chided his host the Pharisee for not having kissed and anointed Jesus too. He invited intimacy with the Samaritan woman at the well (John 4:7), with the woman whose only desire was to touch the hem of his garment (Luke 8:43), with the penitent thief and his grieving mother (John 19:26), even the soldiers who drove the nails of his crucifixion (Luke 23:34). He used his very spittle, alone (Mark 8:23) or mixed with earth (John 9:1), to cure people. There was an unrestrainable largesse to him that can be summed up in the image of the open-armed, welcoming prototype of the quintessential Mediterranean host. This is the Christ most of the New Testament testifies to:* one who embodied a vibrant, unabashed physical life, inclusive and unpredictable, and who was so closely attuned with reality that he broke out of all our familiar human limitations. Being what we call larger than life, he tore open the barrier of finitude by

* Particularly Mark, which was the earliest Gospel and did not have much time to retouch the ardent humanity of Jesus, shows marked physical reactions by Jesus, starting with his normal birth and his adoption by God at his baptism. These include outbursts of anger (3:5, 8:17, 9:19), groans and sighs (8:12), agape for a young man (10:21), despair (15:34), and the marvelous healing of the woman with the flow of blood (5:30).

force of his great uncensored, irrepressible conviction. His resurrection was the ultimate experience of *Being*.*

In light of all this, it is not easily defensible that Christ's church gruesomely focuses on his lurid death, traffics in guilt, and spins our faith into unending cycles of fear, sin, and repentance by worshiping the tormented aspect of Christ's experience. It must be disorienting to pray to a bleeding dead man, naked but for a soiled loincloth, hanging off a cross. Pleading to a tortured God for strength produces an impregnable irony. When monks or theologians speak about contemplating the *beauty* of the dying Christ in church, their usage of the word "beauty" alarms me because it reveals a semiotic distortion that has occurred through our centuries of loving the Augustinian aesthetic of human misery. Our Christianity has come to worship the dead undead, glorifying the afterlife and reenacting the seasonal bloody sacrifice of the god of vegetation like the Egyptians, the Sumerians, or the Minoans before it.† And as the God of the abused, whose ruined body we literally ingest every time we attend Mass, this Christ has come to appeal to our sense of despair.

That is not the Christ of the Last Supper and the miracles, or the risen Lord who ate and drank and invited inspection of his wounds‡; he is not the teacher who grasped the hands of Peter's mother-in-law (Mark 1:31) and of Jairus's daughter (Mark 5:41) and snatched them back from death, the visionary, liberating Messiah whose touch made the blind man see (Mark 8:23) and the bent woman stand upright (Luke 13:13).

---

* "I Am" is the original name of God (Exod. 3:14–15).

† A pharaoh was the son of God too.

‡ The risen Christ says to Mary Magdalene, "Touch me not for I have not yet ascended to my Father" (John 20:17), expecting the possibility of close touch.

The distinctive feature of Christianity is that God became body, and in so doing confirmed and healed our bodily nature. Unlike Zeus or Yahweh, Christ *was* human. And he *used* his body in manifold and sacred ways. His life was an outrage from birth to death. God's becoming flesh was and remains scandalous, and yet its significance has hardly been worked out, mostly because Western Augustinian tradition has so vilified the human body.

At his farewell meal, Christ showed us that, as Parmenides had first revealed, body and knowing are one. He made his teaching physical rather than metaphysical, acted it out in the world of food and drink and dress and skin. He laid his hands on the bread and wine as he had on lepers (Mark 1:41) or children (Mark 10:3), and his touch as always created life, i.e., transformation — because Jesus' living *body* was a tremendous source of intuition and strength. *That* is the strength that is ideally passed on to us through the Eucharist.

We are all — ugly, horny, tired, ditsy, fat, fallen — the body of Christ. That is Christ's unconditional and uncontainable democracy. The taking of the Eucharist is our ritual performance of this union: God and humankind encounter each other in the body. That is the core of the New Testament. Our liberation takes place *in* the body. *That* is our salvation, and our freedom.

Judge Not

Benjamin Cheever

T O be a Christian in polite society is to be a foreigner, an outsider. The confession of faith is greeted with a brilliant smile, a smile that often comes three full seconds too late to be believed. It's as if you had told them about your colostomy bag.

You walk with a mental crutch, you smoke the opiate of the masses. I remember once we had a guest at our house in Pound Ridge, and I decided on the spur of the moment to go to Saint Matthew's in Bedford. My suit was in the room where the guest was sleeping. When I knocked and opened the door, the woman was all smiles. "What do you want a suit for," she asked, "on a Sunday?"

"Church," I said, and tried to look as if it didn't mean anything, my going to church. Still, some instinct for self-preservation caused me to hold the hanger up between us. The woman's face passed through dismay and into stark disapproval. She cast such an unforgiving glance in my direction that when I got back out into a public room, I actually checked the suit pants to see if she had burned a hole in them. I wondered then, I wonder now. What made her furious?

I can see how a taste for conventional religion might be mistaken for foolishness, but why wickedness? Nowadays I go to the nine A.M. service at the Union Church of Pocantico Hills. We don't murder babies. We don't believe in the existence of an international Jewish banking conspiracy.

What does go on, exactly? Well, it's hard to say. We sing. We listen to a sermon. Nine times out of ten the talk is apolitical, although the minister did touch on school prayer recently, declaring himself astounded that anyone seriously thought one person could keep another person from praying, in school or anywhere else for that matter.

Members of the congregation are encouraged to share their griefs and triumphs. We are often asked to pray for the sick, and for those who mourn. I've only spoken once. That was last summer. The running trails in the Rockefeller preserve had been closed because of a drought and the consequent danger of fire. I love to run. I asked for rain.

Seems an innocent way to spend a Sunday morning, so why all this bad feeling? The Moral Majority doesn't help, of course, but I think it's worse than that. I suspect that many people are blaming us for the Bible. In which case I begin to understand. I have trouble with the Bible myself. And I'm talking about the King James Bible. So it's not the language I have trouble with; it's the philosophy I have trouble with.

Fortunately, I didn't come to the Good Book until rather late in life. I didn't have much formal religious education. My father went to church, but my mother did not. So I didn't go to Sunday School a lot. I remember that my suit itched terribly. I remember that we had pea shooters, and there seems to have been one class during which several of the students enlivened the lecture by shooting each other with bits of wadded-up Kleenex. And there were movies. I saw at least three films in which Jesus was played by a gorgeous young man draped in a bed sheet and wearing nothing else but mascara.

My father wrote serious fiction. We had upper-class aspirations. And so we were Episcopalians. Actually, my father's family had been Episcopalian for some time. So I don't know which came first, the class tropism or the religious one. It's a chicken-and-egg situation.

The boys I played with had parents who had emigrated from southern Italy. They went to church every week. They learned jingles, colored in pictures of the Savior's face. Even the toughest kids had to crayon roses in the cheeks of the Son of God. They hated the work. Still, they did it manfully. These boys knew the rules.

The Catholics knew all the rules. They knew the road to paradise. They also knew that I wasn't going to make it. They liked having me around as a sort of a control group, and also as a buffer zone. I was the youngest kid in the gang. Whenever anybody learned a new curse, they'd spell it for me and I'd then say the word out loud. In this way my friends got the double kick of hearing the abomination of choice and also knowing I'd burn for their pleasure. It wasn't as malicious as it sounds; I was ticketed for hell anyway because I ate meat on Fridays and often missed a Sunday service.

I played along with the curse-word drama. I liked the attention. Besides which, I thought I knew that if I kept a pure heart while saying "fuck" and "poontang," and my cynical friends did not keep a pure heart, the Lord would be on my side. I didn't have as much theology as my Catholic friends, but I assumed that God could spell.

In truth, I assumed I knew a good deal more about piety than did my friends. I didn't go to church a lot, but when I did go to church, I would always wear a Brooks Brothers suit. This was the sort of thing God probably took into account. He also would have known that my father wrote for *The New Yorker,* and ate Wheat Thins when he drank his martinis.

The parents of my Catholic playmates ate Velveeta cheese toasted on rounds of Italian bread. They drank wine out of enormous bottles. I knew this because I often went to their apartment and ate their toasted cheese and watched professional wrestling on their television set. I was well aware of the risk I was taking. But then the two families lived very near each other. If there was a flood, I could splash home. We'd get into our Brooks suits, climb into the ark.

I assumed that I'd be saved. I wasn't sure about my friends. I sensed that God wanted men to be kind to each other, and to animals. Especially to animals. I thought God wanted us to be generous and open-minded and to give everybody a second chance. The Golden Rule was his rule, after all. But there were other regulations. Whenever possible, God wanted people to attend an Ivy League college. My Catholic friends had parents who hit them. With belts. My father never hit me. God would like that.

I didn't take a long look at the Bible until I was in my early twenties. I had gotten married, and life had stopped. The adventure was over. I assumed the Bible would be the guidebook for the sort of quiet and excruciating decency I'd rushed into. So I stole a Gideon from a motel. Then I began to read. Big mistake.

I was astonished. It looked like maybe God *was* a Catholic, or something even worse than Catholic. A fascist? Certainly he wasn't kind. Suddenly it was easy to see why Disney never made the movie.

Just take his instructions to Adam and Eve: "And God blessed them, and God said unto them, Be fruitful, and multiply, and fill the earth and subdue it; and have dominion over the fish of the sea, and over the fowl of the air, and over every living thing that moveth upon the earth."

That's what he told them. I can easily see the Sierra Club Foundation having a problem with this. What about endangered species? The population bomb? Pollution? Open spaces?

Then he sets them in the garden of Eden. He tells the young couple that they can't eat from the tree of knowledge of good and evil. He tells them that if they eat of that tree they will surely die. So of course they do eat from that tree. I could see it coming. Couldn't you? Are we supposed to believe that God couldn't see it coming? And then he's sore at them. God loses his temper. Not that they were exactly your model citizens. The first family — they really were the first family — acted like lowlifes, like movie stars. When Adam got caught for having eaten the fruit, he blamed Eve: Eve blamed the snake. They weren't any great shakes as parents, either. One of their sons murdered another one. When God asked Cain about the killing, he lied. He lied to God. Now there's a smart move.

I kept on reading. So far most of the wickedness had been committed by the people, which made sense to me. God was credulous — odd in one who was supposed to be omniscient. But at least he wasn't gratuitously cruel. Or not yet. And of course, I knew that there was something allegorical about these stories. Although it's hard to figure what's allegory and what's direct instruction.

Pretty soon God decided he didn't like anybody but Noah. He warned Noah that there was going to be a flood and that he, Noah, should build a boat. Noah built the ark and took his children aboard. He took two of every animal, except maybe the unicorn. And sure enough, it began to rain.

The ark floated around for a while, and everybody not on it drowned. Everybody and everything. When the water receded, the boat landed. Noah started right in farming. He planted a vineyard. God is central in AA, but it's also important to recall that God was not a teetotaler. Christ didn't turn water into Pellegrino. Noah drank his wine and got drunk. And he was uncovered in his tent. Ham was one of Noah's sons. He was the father of Canaan. Ham went into the tent and "saw the nakedness of his father," I'm quoting exactly here, because otherwise you won't believe me. Ham came out of the tent and told his brothers; they went inside and covered the old guy up. They walked backward, so they didn't see his nakedness. "And Noah awoke from his wine, and knew what his younger son had done to him."

Had done to him? All the kid did was to wander into the tent. Noah was furious. "And he said, Cursed be Canaan; a servant of servants shall he be unto his brethren."

People seeking to justify slavery have since claimed that black people are the sons of Ham. But then if Ham were black, wouldn't Noah have been black as well? That would make us all black. All but the unicorn. In any case, I did think Noah was being a little harsh here. And apparently it was all right with God. Which made me wonder about him too.

In the book of Exodus, God was back with the underdog. Which is a relief. The Egyptians had made his people into slaves. Nobody much sympathizes with Egyptians. The Fertile Crescent seems always to have been a red-light district. They had Cleopatra, and all those bosomy women I saw in the epic films released in the sixties.

Pharaoh was asked to free the Jews. He didn't want to. So God had Moses turn the river blood red and kill all the fish. I hate to think what the Sierra Club would say about that. Still Pharaoh didn't listen. Frogs covered the land. Then gnats. Pharaoh didn't listen. Then God made the livestock sick. Pharaoh didn't listen. Then God covered everybody with boils. Then there was a hailstorm. The modern reader is still with Moses on this one. Then the Lord told Moses, "And all the first-born in the land of Egypt shall die, from the first-born of Pharaoh, who sitteth upon his throne, even unto the first-born of the maidservant who is behind the mill; and all the first-born of the beasts." Now it sounds here like he's lost his temper again.

Then he did it. He actually killed them all. The first-borns. Which I still have trouble with today. Why should God kill the first-born of the maidservant? I thought he had Marxist leanings. And I didn't like at all that he'd killed the animals.

But the Jews were freed. They had been promised a land of milk and honey.

The land, when they reached it, was prime. It was also occupied. By Canaanites. The sons of Ham. Who now had to be gotten rid of. And who were gotten rid of. Why? Because some great, great, great grandfather saw his father's cock? Talk about holding a grudge.

I was outraged. I had gone to the Bible on the assumption that my standards were too low. I seemed to be finding that they were too high instead. And yet the book did have a force well beyond the force of reason. Often when I stumbled on an excerpt, I'd think that I had heard it before. Which I had not done.

I'm not at all clear on the biology of memory. I once read an article about goldfish who were taught a trick, and then when their brains were injected into other, untrained goldfish, the other goldfish also knew the trick. My father's mother was English, and so perhaps I'd inherited parts of the family brain. Generations of forebears dozing in Anglican churches had picked up scraps of Scripture that were passed on to me, along with a taste for gin and a pronounced tendency to melancholy.

Then I started going to church with my father. Church was helpful. Reading the Bible without church is a good deal like taking your Alka Seltzer without water. I had a little family of my own by then, and we found our own church. This was high on a hill in Ossining and presided over by a Father Jack Moody. Father Moody was a man of almost infinite kindness and generosity. If Father Moody had a fault, it was that he was too gentle. I supposed that if Jack Moody could live with the Bible, maybe I could as well. He suggested I read the Gospels. So I began to read the New Testament. Which seemed to be what I had been expecting all along. Only better. Take Luke 6:37: "Judge not, and ye shall not be judged: condemn not, and ye shall not be condemned: forgive, and ye shall be forgiven."

This sounded to me like decent advice. Also it echoed the school-yard jingle "I'm rubber and you're glue; whatever you say bounces off me and sticks to you." And maybe when people judged each other, it would make God angry. Which I knew from the Old Testament was not a good idea. Still, it took me years to realize that this was not simply a regulation but also a piece of wisdom. The mind is highly complicated but also very simple. Go around saying "My parents were thoughtless, selfish, wicked" often enough, and the mind is going to reduce the jingle to "Thoughtless, selfish, wicked." Which is going to become your expectation of a lot of people. And even of yourself.

I've been going to church ever since. First I went six or seven times a year. Now I go most every Sunday. I like seeing men and women bow their heads. I like it when the minister instructs us to be good. Probably we won't be good, but at least somebody has made the suggestion.

C. S. Lewis, in *Mere Christianity,* observed that "First, . . . human beings, all over the earth, have this curious idea that they ought to behave in a certain way, and cannot really get rid of it. Secondly . . . they do not in fact behave in that way. They know the Law of Nature, they break it. These two facts are the foundation of all clear thinking about ourselves and the universe we live in."

This seemed a good reason to be Christian. And as I moved in that direction, I was fascinated by the once-religious people who had lost faith. What did they know that I had missed?

I was terribly impressed with Philip Caputo's novel *Rumor of War.* It sounded to me like the truth. I had read a great many books about Vietnam that had not sounded at all like the truth. I read the book three times. At one point the narrator comes upon the bodies of some dead Vietnamese and decides that he can't believe in a God who would countenance this sort of brutality.

But where is it written that people will not die brutal deaths? Certainly not in the Bible. The Old Testament is a chronicle of horrors. The New Testament is more enlightened than the old one, but neither is it a book without bloodshed. Remember what they did to Christ? It's unthinkable. And so modern man, being so advanced, would rather not think of it. I suspect that many atheists have more trouble with the news of Christ's death than with the assertion of his resurrection.

I admire Philip Caputo. I also admire the people I meet in church. What are we like outside the sanctuary? Do we gladden the hearts of those we love? Are we merciful? I don't know about the others. And it's the beginning of wisdom to admit that I don't even know about myself. And furthermore, that preliminary findings are not good. Perhaps all I really have is a better idea of what to wish for. Which comes from the New Testament. And a better idea of the context in which to have those wishes, which comes from the old one.

CONVENTIONAL religion has lost a good deal of authority in the last two decades. And so the church can bring less force to bear in its moral teachings. And this I sometimes regret. On the other hand, there is a great wrong that is in the process of being corrected.

I grew up in a world in which each church felt that it taught the way, the only way to eternal life. This made sense to me as a child, but I have grown to see it as repugnant in the extreme. This is the same parochialism that justifies war, racism, anti-Semitism, and a host of evils.

A priest or rabbi who has you walk to paradise on the heads of the damned is my idea of a hypocrite. Judge not, and ye shall not be judged. Clergymen with this outlook remind me of the salesman who once came to my door promising a "free gift" if I would buy the Encyclopedia Britannica. Boiled down to its essentials, the message went like this: "Trust me. I'm going to sell you the moral and intellectual heart of Western civilization. But first, I'm going to tell you a lie."

As a child, I assumed that the highest system must be based on manners and class. I think now that this position is at least as mistaken as was the rule-driven spiritual universe of my Catholic playmates. Where we all went wrong was in our confident assumption that others would be damned to hell.

I have never seen anyone excluded from the church I now attend. Not the tourists who come to admire the building and who, when walking forward to receive Communion, cast furtive glances at the stained-glass windows by Chagall. Not the little children who interrupt the sermon with loud questions and complaints. On more than one occasion a tiny worshiper has burst into tears. Sometimes I resent the interruption, and yet even as I resent it, I am aware of my mistake. Christ was very clear in his preference for children. He would have welcomed their noise, cherished their impiety.

The Reverend Paul DeHoff writes a strong sermon. And he has been blessed with a voice that carries.

I find it endlessly heartening to walk up the aisle, look into the pews, and see that when going up to take Communion, the men have often left their car keys unguarded, the women their pocketbooks. Church was once a sanctuary, a place where outcasts and even criminals could save themselves from the mob. And who among us is not a stranger in this world? Man is the lonely, the homesick animal. Homesick when he travels, and homesick when he stays at home.

Paring Off the Amphibologisms
Jesus Recovered by the Jesus Seminar

Lydia Davis

T H E beginning of the path that led me to *The Five Gospels* is as hard to discover as the beginning of a goat- or cow-path in a meadow, but somewhere along the way was a reading of Benjamin Franklin's *Autobiography* and then William Cobbett's utopian descriptions of self-sufficient farming; eventually a videotape in the BBC series *Civilisation* about the eighteenth century and the Enlightenment, specifically the figure of the inventor, the revolutionary, the independent thinker (including the unaccredited amateur versus the professional and academic); and Thomas Jefferson. There was Monticello, which he designed himself, inspired by a French model, the Hôtel de Salm in Paris, and excited particularly by the idea of the one-story facade concealing two stories. There were the farm implements he modernized (he won a gold medal from the Société d'Agriculture du Département de la Seine at Paris for his improved mold-board plow). There was his seven-field crop rotation system. His botanical experiments.

His design for his bedroom and study suite, with his bed in the middle so that he could get out on either side. What characterized him through most of his projects much of the time, it would seem, was confidence in his own abilities and independence of thinking, independence from the norm, the accepted, a readiness to question the received, the conventional. He must have been moved by some dissatisfaction, nonacceptance — dissatisfaction with this conventional desk, with this grand staircase — and also by the pure pleasure in doing the thing himself, in *poiein,* making: his house was always in progress, piles of wood around, treacherous catwalks, and half-lit, narrow stairs. It was this spirit that put him at the center of the declaration of a radical break from England, though it took Thomas Paine's *Common Sense* to convince him, among others, to make the move.

It was in the same spirit that he approached the Bible. Dissatisfied with it as it read, he decided to reduce it "to the simple Evangelists" and even from them to select "the very words only of Jesus," those parts that seemed to him the true teachings of Jesus. He cut passages out of his Bible and pasted them into a blank book to form a coherent *Life and Morals of Jesus* for his own use. This project he carried out while he was president, in the evenings before he went to sleep, and worked on further at Monticello. He was pleased with the result, though reluctant to advertise very widely what he had done. (The Federalists already viewed him as irreligious.) He wrote to a friend, "I am . . . averse to the communication of my religious tenets to the public, because it would countenance the presumption of those who have endeavoured to draw them before that tribunal, and to seduce public opinion to erect itself into that inquest over the rights of conscience, which the laws have so justly proscribed."

Thomas Paine, whose path crossed that of Benjamin Franklin

early in his career (Franklin, who met him in London, advised him to seek his fortune in America) and that of William Cobbett late, became a hero in the United States because of his pamphlet, for which, although he was always out of pocket, he accepted no profits so that cheap editions might be widely circulated. Another independent thinker drawn to invention like Jefferson and Franklin, after the war was over he settled down for a while to designing an iron bridge without piers and a smokeless candle. Then (to abbreviate the story), whereas he had been regarded as a hero for speaking his mind, he began getting into trouble for speaking his mind. In England, in 1791, he published *The Rights of Man,* this time speaking in support of the French Revolution but also of republicanism, outlining a plan for popular education, relief of the poor, pensions for aged people, and public works for the unemployed, all to be financed by the levying of a progressive income tax. The ruling classes found this very threatening and indicted him for treason, but he was already on his way to France. In France, he became involved in the revolution and put himself at risk once again by speaking his mind, this time against the execution of the monarch, thereby antagonizing Robespierre's radicals and causing himself to be thrown into prison.

It was in prison that he wrote the first volume of *The Age of Reason,* an exposition of the place of religion in society and in part a critique of the Bible. He believed in a Supreme Being but did not think Jesus Christ had any divine origin. He did not think the story of Mary and the Holy Ghost was believable. He objected to the barbarity of the Old Testament and questioned the authenticity of the New Testament. He said that "if Christ had meant to establish a new religion, he would have written it down himself." He said in his introduction to the book that he had intended this one to be his last writing because he knew it would make him unpopular, but had started it earlier in his life because of going to prison. He wrote in the preface, "It contains my opinions upon religion. You will do me the justice to remember that I have always strenuously supported the right of every man to his own opinion, however different that opinion might be to mine."

The book did indeed make him very unpopular. He returned to the United States to find that he was widely regarded as the world's greatest infidel. Though he was poor, ill, and given to bouts of drinking, he continued to attack privilege and religious superstitions. (While still in France, he had published another pamphlet, *Agrarian Justice,* that attacked inequalities in property ownership and added to his enemies in establishment circles.) He died lonely and without funds in 1809. Six people attended his funeral. (His bones were later exhumed by William Cobbett, in fact, who took them to England with the intention of giving them a proper funeral; on the way, however, he lost them.) For more than a century following his death he continued to be thought of in the terms of his obituary — as one who "did some good and much harm."

THE Five Gospels: The Search for the Authentic Words of Jesus, by Robert W. Funk, Roy W. Hoover, and the Jesus Seminar — a group of biblical scholars led by Funk and John Dominic Crossan — appeared in 1993. It is dedicated to Thomas Jefferson, among others, and, as Jefferson and Paine did, it takes a fresh look at the Bible, specifically the four Gospels of the New Testament along with a fifth, the Gospel of Thomas. Like Jefferson and Paine, it also takes a risk thereby — laying itself open to a negative reaction from public opinion and the establishment. In fact, at least one of the scholars in the Jesus Seminar lost his university position as a result of this work, and others were forced to withdraw from the project as a consequence of institutional pressure. One difference, though, is that this is a work of critical scholarship and at various times has involved between thirty and two hundred scholars (seventy-four are listed in the roster at the back of the book).

Along with the commentated Gospels of Mark, Matthew, Luke, John, and Thomas, *The Five Gospels* contains various front matter and various back matter, including an "Index of Red & Pink Letter Sayings," and is supplemented throughout with other matter, including chronologies, figures, and "cameo essays" clarifying certain points or issues. One, for instance, compares versions of the Lord's Prayer with interesting results.

As described in its preface, this is the collective report of Gospel scholars working together on a common question: What did Jesus really say? The scholars "first of all inventoried all the surviving ancient texts for words attributed to Jesus. They then examined those words in the several ancient languages in which they have been preserved. They produced a translation of all the gospels, known as the Scholars Version. And, finally, they studied, debated, and voted on each of the more than 1,500 sayings of Jesus in the inventory."

A number of different factors, or "rules of evidence," as the seminar calls them, come into play in determining which words in all likelihood originated with Jesus himself and were handed down from the time of the oral tradition into the written tradition, and which words were editorial or storytellers' additions contributed by the evangelists themselves.

Nothing extant was written down during Jesus' lifetime. Thus, only what could have been transmitted orally from Jesus' time, only what was memorable for one reason or another, easily memorized, can be proved to have been Jesus' words or close to them. "Only sayings and parables that can be traced back to the oral period, 30–50 C.E., can possibly have originated with Jesus." For this reason, when there are many versions of a saying or parable, usually the briefest and simplest will be the oldest one, the one closest to the original. Also, a parable may reveal evidence of mnemonic techniques common in oral literature — triadic structures and the repetition of catchwords — and thus be more likely to have been handed down from the oral period.

A storyteller will tend to supply dialogue appropriate to the occasion, putting words in Jesus' mouth that would not have been handed down independently from the oral period, and those additions can be spotted and identified as the contributions of the storyteller. The first narrative Gospel, the Gospel of Mark, was not written until about 70 C.E. It was preceded (50–60 C.E.) by "sayings" gospels — i.e., gospels that did not embed sayings and parables within a narrative. The names of the authors of the four Gospels in the New Testament are names made up and assigned to them. It is not known what their actual names were. Surviving fragments of other, unknown gospels indicate that there were once many gospels. About twenty are known, and there may be many more.

A comparison of Gospels texts in which parables are recounted will reveal a core parable that may have been handed down from the oral period. Likewise, similar material coming from different sources will imply that the material existed independently at an earlier time. Stylistic analysis of a single Gospel will reveal habits of thought or flourishes characteristic of one evangelist (e.g., Mark's attitude toward Jesus' disciples, Matthew's fondness for the phrase "in the heavens") that can then be pared away.

An example of a comparison of texts would be setting side by side the two accounts of Jesus' dictation of the Lord's Prayer, one in Matthew and one in Luke. When we take away editorial emendations by the evangelists, such as "who art in heaven," which was one of Matthew's favorite phrases and one that does not appear in Luke, we are left with a form of four petitions that Jesus probably did address to God, though not assembled into a single prayer: that the name of the Father be revered, and that he impose his imperial rule, provide daily bread, and forgive debts. The only word, however, that we can be certain Jesus spoke is the opening word, "Father," or *Abba* in Aramaic. Curiously, because of what we cannot be sure he said, the one word he surely said, *Abba,* acquires tremendous force.

A consideration of the historical context in which the Gospels were written — the early years of the evolving Christian movement — will reveal still more about the ideological bias or proselytizing tendency of the evangelist and influence our reading of a Gospel. For instance, Luke, unlike Matthew, omits Jesus' admonition "When anyone conscripts you for one mile, go an extra mile." Since his Gospel was a defense of the Christian movement for Roman consumption, he may have omitted the admonition for fear that it would offend the Romans, who were probably the ones doing the conscripting. Another instance: parables involving masters leaving and returning were especially popular with the evangelists because they foreshadowed the later accounts of Jesus' leaving and returning, and so have to be examined with particular vigilance.

As they searched for the authentic words of Jesus, members of the seminar had to go on the assumption that his voice was distinctive in a crowd of Galileans that included other sages. A sage was a repository for received wisdom, free-floating proverbs, witticisms of the time. Some of this commonly accepted wisdom of the time may have been attributed to Jesus by the evangelists, and some of it may in fact have been repeated by him. Since it is not distinctive, we can't know. For instance, one of the evangelists has Jesus say, "Be at peace with one another," but this was a common sentiment that nearly everyone uttered at one time or another, so one can't say these were Jesus' words.

The Five Gospels is a color-coded report of the results of these deliberations. In red are printed "words that were most probably spoken by Jesus in a form close to the one preserved for us." Bold black signals that "Jesus did not say this; it represents the perspective or content of a later or different tradition." The remaining two colors, pink and blue gray, signal positions in between the two extremes: "Jesus probably said something like this"; and "Jesus did not say this, but the ideas contained in it are close to his own." The color-coded Gospels "answer the question 'What did Jesus really say?' within a narrow range of historical probabilities."

The book does not specifically promise that a portrait of Jesus will emerge, but of course it does, through the sifting of texts to discover what Jesus probably said, because the more we learn about the expressive style of the man, the more we learn about the personality and character of the man.

Until just a few months ago, for me the figure of Jesus had been so painted and repainted with layers of dogma, inflation, sentimentality, hypocrisy, prejudice, deception, that what might or might not lie beneath — the historical figure, the sage of Nazareth — was wholly obscured. The very words traditionally associated with Jesus, including most of all the name Jesus itself, carried a burden of association that tended to close my ears before speech began. I see this in some others still, if I mention Jesus or the words of Jesus — or perhaps it is not that ears are closed but what is expressed by the Mandarin verb construction *ting bu jian,* "one listens but fails to hear." ("Anyone here with two good ears had better listen!" is a traditional refrain that appears regularly in the Gospels, especially following parables and sayings that were difficult to understand. It cannot be proved that Jesus himself actually said it.) The words of Jesus appear everywhere all the time in this culture: a reference to "turning the other cheek" (which it seems Jesus probably did advise) on a poster in a veterinarian's examining room showing a kitten being licked by a puppy; a reference to shaking the dust from one's feet in a comic strip in the Sunday paper ("And whatever place does not welcome you or listen to you, get out of there and shake the dust off your feet in witness against them" [Mark 6:11] is concluded by the Jesus Seminar not to have originated with Jesus but to have been a vindictive response by early missionaries). But the figure of Jesus that keeps appearing to us in this culture turns out to be in certain of his aspects unlike the historical Jesus, or unlike the Jesus that emerges in *The Five Gospels* "within a narrow range of historical probabilities."

Jesus wrote nothing, so far as we know. We do not know for certain that Jesus could write; we are not even positive that he could read. His native tongue was Aramaic. We do not know whether he could speak Hebrew as well. His words have been preserved only in Greek, the original language of all the surviving Gospels. However, it is possible that Jesus also spoke Greek, in which case some parts of the oral tradition preserved in the Gospels may have originated with him. (Sometimes, as in Mark's account of the raising of Jairus's daughter, Jesus' purported words were quoted, within the Greek Gospel, in the original Aramaic, possibly for the reason that to readers of the Greek, the Aramaic *talitha koum* would sound like a magical formula, whereas it simply means "Little girl, get up!")

Jesus was a carpenter.

Jesus was probably a disciple of John the Baptist.

Jesus was a sage, a wandering sage, a wandering charismatic. In his wanderings he was frequently accompanied by followers.

Many of Jesus' followers started as disciples of John the Baptist.

He apparently abided by these rules while traveling: not to carry a knapsack, bread (food), a purse (money), or a second shirt (change of clothes). Not to move around town once arrived, but to stay under one roof. He may have worn sandals and carried a staff. The staff and sandals would have been concessions to road conditions. More stringent would have been no staff and no sandals. (Another clue in the detective work of the Jesus Seminar was that early followers of Jesus were likely to be more severe in their asceticism than either Jesus himself or later followers.) The guiding principle was to trust in the provisions of providence.

He paid little attention to food and clothing, except what was required for the day. His petition in the Lord's Prayer — "Provide us with the bread we need for the day" (Matt. 6:11) — would therefore have been characteristic. (Luke expanded this from the single day to a more extended future by adding "day by day.") He advised that others disregard food and clothing, as other sages also advised.

But he and his disciples did not fast. On the contrary, he apparently liked to eat and drink and probably enjoyed weddings. Among some people, he had a reputation as a "glutton and a drunk" (Luke 7:34).

He probably did exorcise what were thought to be demons. But like other sages of the time, he did not offer to cure people. People seeking his help either petitioned in person or had someone petition for them.

He rarely initiated dialogue or debate. Rather, he responded. (This sometimes provides another clue in the search: when he is made to initiate a dialogue, these are probably not his words.)

He was, like other sages of the ancient Near East, laconic, slow to speech, a person of few words.

He was self-effacing, modest, unostentatious. He urged humility as the cardinal virtue by both word and example. He admonished his followers to be self-effacing.

He tended to focus attention away from himself and on God instead.

He rarely made pronouncements or spoke about himself in the first person.

He made no claim to be the Anointed, the Messiah. He probably did not think of his work as a program he was carrying out. He was not an institution builder. (He was not a Christian, of course, but he was made to talk like a Christian by the evangelists.)

He taught on his own authority, characteristically making his points by parables and aphorisms, not apparently invoking Scripture.

Jesus' public discourse was remembered to have consisted primarily of aphorisms, parables, and retorts to challenges.

The flat refusal, the unqualified statement, was characteristic of Jesus.

Jesus frequently indulged in repartee. He was a master of enigmatic repartee. For instance, when asked by some Pharisees and Herodians whether they should pay a poll tax to the Roman emperor, he does not advise them either way but says simply, "Pay the emperor what belongs to the emperor, and God what belongs to God" (Mark 12:17).

His sayings and stories, because enigmatic, were readily misunderstood and often provoked a strong negative response.

He challenged the everyday, the inherited, the established. He undermined a whole way of life. He endorsed countermovements and ridiculed established traditions.

He was antisocial. He erased social boundaries taken to be sacrosanct. He was sympathetic to those who were marginal to society or outcasts. He associated freely with outcasts (e.g., sinners — meaning nonobservant Judeans — and toll collectors). He rejected the notion that ritual impurity could result from contact with lepers, the dead, or gentiles. (The rabbis held that heathen dust was polluting and therefore made Judeans ritually unclean.) He felt that impurity could come only from within. "Listen to me, all of you, and try to understand! It's not what goes into a person from the outside that can defile; rather, it's what comes out of the person that defiles" (Mark 7:14–15, Scholars Version). (King James Version: "Hearken unto me every one of you, and understand: there is nothing from without a man, that entering into him can defile him: but the things which come out of him, those are they that defile the man.") He had in general a relaxed attitude toward the Law.

He confused the distinction between insiders and outsiders. He believed that God's domain belonged to the poor. (The early, Palestinian Christian community was essentially a movement of poor peasants. Many abandoned family ties, property, social position, in response to his summons.) He took a more liberal view of women and the status of women than was usual in the patriarchal society of the time.

Jesus' sayings and parables cut against the social and religious grain (as, for instance, "Love your enemies" [Luke 6:27]). They surprised and shocked: they characteristically called for a reversal of roles or frustrated ordinary, everyday expectations.

He turned expectations on their head. "What does God's imperial rule remind me of? It is like leaven which a woman took and concealed in fifty pounds of flour until it was all leavened" (Luke 13:20–21). Shocking, because leaven at that time was customarily regarded as a symbol of corruption and evil.

He spoke often about God's imperial rule. But he spoke of it as already present, not in apocalyptic terms. (It was Mark's habit to speak in apocalyptic terms.) He conceived of it as all around but difficult to discern, close or already present but unobserved. (Evidence of this lies in Jesus' major parables, which do not reflect an apocalyptic view of history: e.g., Samaritan, prodigal son, dinner party, vineyard laborers, shrewd manager, unforgiving slave, corrupt judge, leaven, mustard seed, pearl, treasure.)

God was so real for him that he could not distinguish God's present activity from any future activity. He had a sense of time in which the future and the present merged, in the intensity of his vision.

Jesus' sayings and parables are often characterized by paradox, as in "Love your enemies." Those who love their enemies have no enemies. Or: "Do good, and lend, expecting nothing in return" (Luke 6:35). Lending without expectation of repayment is not lending. Or: "You must be as sly as a snake and as simple as a dove" (Matt. 10:16). To adopt the posture of the snake and the dove at the same time is a contradiction.

Whereas his followers were more serious-minded, Jesus tended to employ comic hyperbole, graphic exaggeration, as in the following: "It's easier for a camel to squeeze through a needle's eye than for a wealthy person to get into God's domain" (Mark 10:25). As *The Five Gospels* explains, "This saying presented difficulties to the Christian community from the very beginning. Some Greek scribes substituted the Greek word rope (*kamilon*) for the term camel (*kamelon*) to reduce the contrast, while some modern but misguided interpreters have claimed that the 'needle's eye' was the name of a narrow gate or pass, which a camel would find difficult, but not impossible, to pass through."

Jesus' sayings and parables are often characterized by exaggeration, humor, and paradox combined. In the parable of the mustard seed, for instance, Jesus compares God's domain to the lowly mustard weed. He uses the image of the mustard weed as a parody of Ezekiel's mighty cedar of Lebanon and the apocalyptic tree of Daniel, traditional images for God's domain at that time. Jesus is poking fun at the symbol of the mighty tree that prevailed. But the evangelists were swayed by that same symbol to try and bring Jesus' metaphor closer to it. "What is God's imperial rule like? What does it remind me of? It is like a mustard seed which a man took and tossed into his garden. It grew and became a tree, and the birds of the sky roosted in its branches" (Luke 13:18–19). (King James Version: "Unto what is the kingdom of God like? and whereunto shall I resemble it? It is like a grain of mustard seed, which a man took, and cast into his garden; and it grew, and waxed a great tree; and the fowls of the air lodged in the branches of it.")

Many of Jesus' sayings and parables employ a concrete natural image, as for instance: locust, rooster, snake, fish, dove, sparrow, crow, fox, camel, shirt, coat, belt, hand, foot, cheek, hair, eye, city, marketplace, synagogue, house, lamp, lamp stand, jar, couch, seat, needle, bushel basket, grape, wine, wineskin, vineyard, salt, leaven, dough, bread, meal, seed, grain, sickle, harvest, sun, rain, dust, mountain, stone, pearl, coin, timber, sliver, bramble, thorn, thistle, reed, slave, master, doctor, beggar, bailiff, judge, emperor, bridegroom, toll collector. The concrete image is exploited in a surprising and unusual way, as for instance: "Figs are not gathered from thorns, nor are grapes picked from brambles" (Luke 6:44).

Jesus often raised questions from a literal to a metaphorical level. His sayings and parables were customarily metaphorical and without explicit application. Because his parables were told in figurative language, because the figures could not be taken literally, because the application of the saying was left ambiguous, what he said was difficult to understand, and the disciples often did not know what he was saying. (Mark made the disciples out to be stupid, this was one of his particular biases, and it is he who has Jesus say such things to his disciples as: "Are you as dimwitted as the rest?") But Jesus did not explain. Instead, he gave them more questions, more stories with unclear references. The answer shifted the decision back onto his listeners. Jesus' style was to refuse to give straightforward answers.

Jesus emphasized reciprocity. ("Forgive and you'll be forgiven" [Luke 6:37].)

Jesus spoke out against divorce.

Jesus gave injunctions difficult for early communities to practice (such as "Love your enemies," and such as the injunction against divorce).

He may have realized the potential danger he incurred by challenging the status quo.

During a meal, Jesus might very likely have engaged in some

symbolic acts. He probably made use of bread or fish and wine. (Bread and fish were the staples of the Galilean diet.)

It is possible that one of the disciples betrayed Jesus and that Jesus may have become aware of that betrayal.

Jesus did not speculate about the appearance of the Messiah in the last days or about counterfeit messiahs and false prophets.

ANOTHER saying or parable characterized by exaggeration, or hyperbole, is the following: "That's why I tell you: don't fret about life — what you're going to eat — or about your body — what you're going to wear. Remember, there is more to living than food and clothing. . . . Think about how the lilies grow: they don't slave and they never spin. Yet let me tell you, even Solomon at the height of his glory was never decked out like one of these" (Luke 12:22–28). The exaggeration: human beings are not given clothing by God in the same way that lilies are clothed.

The King James Version of this passage reads: "Therefore I say unto you, Take no thought for your life, what ye shall eat; neither for the body, what ye shall put on. The life is more than meat, and the body is more than raiment. . . . Consider the lilies how they grow: they toil not, they spin not; and yet I say unto you, that Solomon in all his glory was not arrayed like one of these."

The Scholars Version has the ring of "translationese" to it, an effect partly of colliding dictions (the slangy "decked out" sits unhappily in the same sentence as the more formal and archaic "one of these" — and numerous other examples of these unhappy marriages can be found throughout the translation) and partly of "wooden ear" choices, such as the pairing of "Yet let." There are, further, rhythmical deficiencies that make it far less generally euphonious than the King James Version, though it is undoubtedly more accurate and based on a more accurate version of the original text.

"Consider the lilies how they grow" sings to us more than "Think about how the lilies grow" for several reasons having to do with rhythm: in the first line, the scansion of the multisyllabic iambic "consider" propels the line forward, and the two-syllable "lilies" continues the momentum, whereas "Think about" stops the line short; we stumble over the awkward rhymed pair of "about how," and the monosyllables "how the" slow the motion further, so that the concluding "lilies grow" sounds flat and unexciting. The sentence as a whole is rhythmically disorganized. In the King James Version the line is divided by a perceptible caesura into two three-word phrases with alliterated middle words, "Consider the lilies" and "how they grow," that could conceivably stand alone — "consider   the   lilies!   how   they   grow!" — which creates a pleasing balance, the caesura giving a gentle emphasis to the word "lilies." This balance of paired phrases is echoed in the more closely parallel pair that immediately follows — "they toil not, they spin not" — and in fact maintained through the entire passage quoted above, from just after the opening "Therefore I say unto you" until the concluding "and yet I say unto you," when the departure from the pattern heightens the eloquence of the closing declaration. But in the Scholars Version the balanced structures so precisely maintained in the King James Version are often either slightly lopsided — "they toil not, they spin not" becomes "they don't slave and they never spin" — or abandoned altogether — "The life is more than meat, and the body is more than raiment" becomes "there is more to living than food and clothing." Other rhetorical devices — repetition, alliteration, assonance — that are deployed in the King James Version to further tie the passage together may be absent or seem almost accidental in the Scholars Version.

But I find that when I turn to the King James Version for comparison, beautiful though it is, my ears often cease to hear. It is hard to tell what it is that closes my ears: whether it is the familiarity of the King James Version, or its association with an inaccessible Jesus figure, or its lyricism. It may be that the words of this translation are so well known by now that they cease to convey anything; certainly they convey nothing fresh coming from a newly perceived Jesus. It may be that the somewhat antique flavor of the language further distances the thoughts from us. It is hard to measure just how much attention the very beauty of the language attracts to itself and distracts from the thoughts it expresses. In any case, my attention is in fact turned less effectively to the substance of Jesus' thought in the King James Version than in the more modest Scholars Version — just as the modest (and terse) Jesus himself tended to direct attention away from himself and toward God (unlike some of his proselytizers). The result, oddly, is that the very difficulty of the Scholars Version — the constant jolts, the rockiness — has a tonic effect: it keeps me awake, or keeps the text awake; it refreshes it, allows me to hear it.

Despite the less euphonious translation of Jesus' words, the words are still compelling, probably for several reasons: the surprising thoughts they express, the inherent interest of the thoughts, and the way they are expressed, through striking, concrete images that tie the thoughts to everyday objects that are closely, physically connected to us. These are some of the very same reasons that Jesus' statements were compelling in the first place.

*   *   *

THE paradoxical effect of putting Jesus back into his historical context, among other sages and wandering charismatics of his time, is that he, through the style of his language, and through what it reveals of his character and his thought, becomes newly outstanding. The effect of the Jesus Seminar's patient, "critical" detective work in what Jefferson called "paring off the amphibologisms" is to reveal Jesus more fully than he was revealed before. Where skepticism clears the way, there is room for belief.

The "final general rule of evidence" of the Jesus Seminar is: "Beware of finding a Jesus entirely congenial to you."

Finding him congenial, here, would mean seeing him as you want to see him, seeing him as your preconceived notions would have you see him, distorting or skewing what you see into what you want to see.

This was the seminar's protective amulet against bias, against obfuscation, against muddy thinking. It's a wonderful recommendation that one might advisedly adopt as one's own guiding principle in life, with certain substitutions: beware of finding a native land entirely congenial to you; beware of finding an ideology entirely congenial to you; beware of finding a leader entirely congenial to you.

It occurred to me as I made my way here and there along these paths of history that there is a joy in independence, in the risk of independence in one's thinking and making, and there is joy even in contemplating the works of the independent thinker. But what also occurred to me is that there is safety, reassurance, in being an uncritical follower, especially of an independent thinker, a revolutionary, especially of a newly discovered independent thinker or revolutionary, and that the challenge to the follower, consequently, is to remain independent in turn — even of those we admire, of those who are themselves independent. That is, to continue to look with clear eyes, with the eyes of the "critical scholar," at Jefferson, at Paine, at Jesus, at the Jesus Seminar. For fear that otherwise we have eyes but do not look. Or maybe it should be: we look but do not see.

The Magnificat

Coco Fusco

T H E Bible? A quote from Scripture that would organize my thoughts? At first, I draw a blank. Ask me about the power of people's faith. Ask me about how faith can transform, how religion serves as a repository for the utopian aspirations of the oppressed. Ask me how a book that was imposed on Latin America by force has become one of the continent's most subversive texts. Ask me about the liberation theology some missionaries told me about when I was still a textbook Marxist who thought she was a character in a Godard film. Or ask me to confess that I began to love art because of the paintings and statues and stained-glass windows that kept me entertained during Mass when I was a kid.

I only heard snippets of the Bible at church as a child. In truth, it was really movies like *The King of Kings* and *The Ten Commandments* that helped me put the pieces together while cajoling me into imagining that God made himself manifest through a series of less-than-perfect special effects. My father's sister, who was a cloistered nun for the last four decades of her life, sent me dozens of rosaries, prayer cards, and pictures of saints while I was growing up — but I don't recall ever receiving a Bible from her. Thanks to TV movies, my illustrated Children's Missal, and the deliciously melodramatic paraphernalia that the Catholic

Church had to offer, I spent my early years swimming in religion without ever having to read the great book myself.

I am not sure if this initial resistance to speaking of the Bible as an unequivocal believer comes from having seen too many fanatics on the streets of New York reciting scriptural verses at a frenzied pitch, or from vestiges of skepticism from my days as a resolute secularist, or even from the old Catholic view that lay-people needed priests to interpret the Bible for them. Whatever the cause, going to the Bible on my own, to reflect upon it in solitude, doesn't feel right for me. I am the first to admit that those who are immersed in religious belief in childhood are stuck with that socialization for the rest of their lives — I know I can't completely shed mine, nor will any other faith ever feel as natural to me as Catholicism has. Nonetheless, I would not treat any text that has had such a far-reaching social and political impact on the world as if it were something that could be looked at in isolation. Believe in the Bible or not, all I can know of it, quips the post-modern intellect in me, but Scripture's real impact lies in its mul-tifarious enunciations in history — enunciations by people.

Even before I could draw a theoretical line between knowl-edge and belief, I had already been primed by my father to watch out for claims that were made in the name of the Bible. The more devout Catholic of my parents, he insisted on distinguishing be-tween a Christian ethics of charity and the church, in all its rich-ness, as a self-interested institution. He could open a clinic for poor immigrants under the auspices of the Catholic archdiocese and at the same time stomp out of the splendid churches we visited on trips to Spain and Italy, disgusted by the discrepancy between the ostentatious wealth housed within and the squalor outside. And then there were my mother's acerbic comments about how Sunday Mass was nothing more than a fashion show for the local elite of the small Cuban town of her youth. Later came her bitterness over our neighborhood church's lack of concern at my father's sudden death and her early widowhood. Though I don't remember paying much attention to what the grown-ups said, the skepticism that underlay their outward respect for the word of God was passed down to me. Decades later, I am still split between one side of me that is fascinated by the creative expressions of devotion and the other side that casts a critical eye upon the relation between faith and action in the world.

Perhaps it is because I trace my roots to parts of the globe where the Catholic Church has rarely played an active role in challenging entrenched social inequities that I am so impressed by those who have been inspired by the Gospel to fight to secure basic human rights. In the back of my mind, I can see the priests who turned their churches into sanctuaries for Central Americans fleeing death squads in the 1980s. I remember Father Pat, a Chicano priest I met years ago in the San Luis Valley of Colorado, who was repatriating exquisite wood-carved *santos* back to local churches and assisting Native American activists in the protection of sacred sites from strip-mining. I think of Bishop Samuel Ruiz, who has mediated negotiations between the Zapatistas in the Lacandon jungle and the Mexican ruling party. These are people, I tell myself, whose faith compels them to intervene in human dramas on behalf of the disempowered. They take real risks because they read the Bible, as theologian Gustavo Gutierrez put it, as a call for "prophetic denunciation of dehumanizing situations."

But then I say to myself that I am lapsing into the tendency I've criticized others for, searching far away rather than looking at the realities right in front of my face. Don't I remember that it was in my worst moment of agony as an adult, when my brother was killed in 1984, that I felt the embrace of a community of faith? Didn't I take comfort in praying for nine nights with the nuns who sat around my family's table? Don't I remember listening to my cousin, who at the time was about to be ordained as an Episcopal priest, say to my mother from the pulpit, "Julia, tú conoces el dolor de la madre de Dios." ("Julia, you know the pain that the mother of God also felt.") Those are the only words I can remember from the day of the funeral.

My cousin Cathy had converted to Episcopalianism some years before and shortly after her conversion entered seminary. She was my favorite relative from my father's side of the family, a former actress and theater director with an infectious laugh. She was the female kin I most admired, the only one in whom I perceived a truly independent spirit. I could tell from the way she talked about her time in seminary that her theological vision was feminist without being exclusionary, and I could sense from the way she spoke and the company she kept that she was part of a progressive force within the Anglican Church. Her first job after her ordination was running a soup kitchen at Holy Apostles Church in Chelsea, where she tended to thousands of homeless people every week. I don't remember ever having a conversation with other family members about what Cathy was up to, but I secretly suspected that her embrace of a Christian sense of mission had an enormously humbling effect on the rest of us. I may have wondered from time to time about the significance of religious conversion, or what it meant culturally for someone from my family of garrulous Cubans and Italians to find a home in the Church of England, but I could not help but admire the purity of Cathy's faith. Had anyone else in my family made such a decisive move, it might not have made as deep an impression. But Cathy was the relative I considered closest to me in spirit; she was the other rebel daughter, the other intellectual, the other artist — and probably the only kin who could bring me to address the nature of my own religious conviction.

To her credit, Cathy has never tried to force me to follow her path. Unlike my aunt, the nun, or other pious relatives, she never used guilt as a means of persuasion. Instead, she invited me to become godmother to her daughter, and through that bond enabled me to affirm a commitment to both family and faith — by *doing* something that I actually wanted to do. No other role I've played has caused me to think more about spirituality, or its connection to a fundamentally human need to give and receive love. If that can be read as an affirmation of my own faith, then so be it. I look upon it as my cousin's gift.

Though it seemed at one time that Cathy's capacity for charity was boundless, I knew it hit her hard to witness how cruel the city we both grew up in was becoming toward its most unfortunate. In those few moments when she could turn off her automatic problem-solver switch, the magnitude of the human tragedies she was confronting began to make her reflect on the significance of her efforts. One day she told me that she wasn't sure if the service she was providing through the church wasn't making it easier for the state to ignore the problems of widespread poverty and hunger. Soon, she left to move to San Francisco with her husband and daughter.

A year ago, in 1995, she called to tell me that she had been nominated to become the first woman bishop in New York State. In January, amid a flurry of media hype, she was consecrated at the Cathedral of Saint John the Divine in what has to be one of the most spectacular ceremonies I've ever witnessed. Seven hundred and fifty people carrying banners from different churches gave the event an air of medieval pageantry. We were greeted by Japanese drummers and led out by African dancers, serenaded by a rock band, and read to in Chinese, Spanish, and sign language. Two of Cathy's colleagues engaged in a dialogue sermon that touched on feminism, homophobia, and the history of missionary involvement in the colonization of the American West. Cathy's radiant daughter, now on the threshold of womanhood, grinned as she read a passage from the Bible about good family relations that made the congregation of four thousand titter.

Later, I told my cousin that I had been amazed to hear people laugh during a reading from the Bible. In that collective outburst, sparked by an awareness of how the text could come alive, and how it could mean something poignant, ironic, or uncannily real, I heard how a community could form, re-form, and affirm itself through its interaction with Scripture. In the silence that filled the room while lengthy passages were read in languages other than English, I felt a respectfulness for others that went beyond perfunctory politeness. I watched with the absolute attentiveness of one who was taking in something momentous for the very first time; I saw how Cathy had adapted a tradition and turned it into a joyous vision of diversity and inclusiveness. Attuned to the politics of space, she set herself in the middle of it all, insisting that the liturgy be carried out at the crossing, at the edge of the congregation, rather than from the high altar. "It would have been too distant, and not congruent with my approach to ministry," she said afterward in a long conversation we had at her new home. "It is the gathering of the people that is sacred."

I can't say this was the only sort of religious ceremony I've witnessed in which I could feel the power of people's faith. On the contrary, what moved me was how close it seemed to the sacredness of communal gatherings in other cultures; to the kinetic invocation of Yoruba saints in Afro-Cuban *toque santos,* for example, or to the Dakota philosophy that speech shared among a group is the actualization of the spirit. This in itself was the surprise — a collective sense of the sacred with a performative, expansive approach to Scripture was hardly what I would have expected in an Episcopalian cathedral in Manhattan.

Nor could I have anticipated how cultural diversity would manifest itself in this arena. For instead of treating the non-Anglo of the service as exotic imports that were to compensate for a lack of expressiveness, Cathy structured the consecration as a chorus of ecstatic voices, not always in harmony, but consistently in concert. Wasn't it my cousin's particularly special grace, I thought to myself, to have presided over an event in which four thousand people could be so genuinely pleased to join?

"Tradition is a living thing," she explained as we sat surrounded by books, family pictures, and her beloved dogs, who, I could have sworn, were reincarnations of the perky little terriers she'd had when I was a kid. "We need to translate [tradition] into languages that different people can respond to. But we also must look at issues of power. Too often when we reach out, we want the new people, but we want them to be like us. That doesn't work."

One of Cathy's new concerns as a bishop in Westchester County was to deal with a dramatic rise in the region's Latino congregation. I was intrigued by the political implications of that demographic shift. It set my mind at ease to know that Latino immigrants seeking a church willing to open itself to them might opt for a more liberal haven than the fundamentalisms now sweeping through a region that was once solidly Catholic territory. I had a feeling that behind Cathy's demographic lay the failure of the largely Irish Catholic hierarchy in the United States to accommodate believers from the southern hemisphere. But my own memories of having had to play the token ethnic in a sea of white faces made me wonder what it would be like for them.

"You know how it is when people start wanting to get to know members of other cultures — how they start trying their food, and then want to know about their traditions?" Cathy said to me (with just a hint of sarcasm). "Well, that's the wrong way of going about things." As a preemptive strike against the more conventional approach to multiculturalism, which, according to her view, would have allowed the dominant group to remain normative, she had already proposed a diversity awareness program for the majority Anglo parishioners. "The church needs to live out the Kingdom as a vision of mutuality" was her way of explaining her strategy.

I had sent Cathy a letter some weeks before, asking her if I could interview her about her work. I hadn't told her specifically that I was looking for a way into a discussion of the Bible, but in response to my query, she sent me her first sermon as a bishop, which began with the Magnificat. This passage from Luke tells the story of Mary and her older cousin Elisabeth, both of whom find themselves with child — miraculously, for Elisabeth is old and was apparently barren, and Mary's conception is "immaculate." When Mary arrives, Elisabeth feels the baby move in her womb and recognizes instantly that Mary is about to become the mother of Christ. Mary answers her cousin's recognition of her state with a song of praise to her savior for choosing her, a poor woman, to be the one whom "henceforth all generations will call . . . blessed."

There are so many things I liked about this passage when I

first read it that it's difficult to know where to begin. That it would be a woman with child who could recognize a similar state in another, and rejoice in the significance of their condition, strikes me as an incredibly earthy way of dramatizing the beginning of a prophetic transformation of the world. I can imagine the two cousins together in joyful conversation, and I smile inwardly at the fact that this portentous moment takes place while, on the one hand, Elisabeth's husband has been struck dumb for doubting the angel's message, and on the other, Mary's fiancé, Joseph, is not in her company. There's a kind of folk wisdom in these lines that draws me in. Isn't that how unbelievable things usually happen?

Most of the Magnificat, however, has little to do with their pregnancies per se. Instead it celebrates creation's link to a principle of transformation. As I confront the passage, I stop for a minute to try to figure out whether this passage might not be the origin of the use of pregnancy as a symbol for human creativity that would later be taken up by such masterful painters as Vermeer. It's as if Mary herself draws one away from a literal reading, indicating with the substance of her utterance that her pregnancy is at once real and a metaphor. Rather than focusing on her condition in the Magnificat, she sings about a merciful God who provides for the poor and hungry: (Luke 1:52–53)

> He has scattered the proud in the imagination of their hearts, he hath put down the mighty from their thrones, and exalted those of low degree; he has filled the hungry with good things, and the rich he has sent empty away.

Here is the voice of the subaltern, so sought after by postcolonial theorists. Mary is a humble Middle Eastern Jew who is unmarried and pregnant, and she doesn't sound too worried about it. A Marxist would say she is discoursing on the dialectics of history. A feminist might point out that she's foreshadowing the ethical principle that forms the basis of her son's credo. I look at it and think, If there is any message in the Bible I'd want to believe is true, it would be this one. I've spent enough time in polarized societies that experience drastic shifts in wealth and power on a regular basis to know that people who live in them often hold onto such ideas as an expression of hope and their sense of justice. Liberation theologians have singled out this ode to the reversal of fortune as one of the New Testament's most important messages regarding political change. It was sung at Cathy's consecration, and she read it again for her first sermon as bishop.

Invoking the Magnificat was Cathy's way of explaining how her own prior professional marginalization within the church had actually turned out to benefit her in preparing for her new role. I heard the feminist theologian in her as she likened her election, as a woman, to the removal of a sword from the Virgin Mary's heart. "For before tonight she who made Christ present in the world would not have been permitted to make Christ present at your altar," she had proclaimed at the Church of Saint Mary the Virgin.

I had been struck upon reading her sermon at how able she was to render the human dimension of biblical verse. I felt no distance between the spiritual, the historical past, and the present realities that she wove together in her writings and her way of reflecting on life. How was she able to do it?

"The enterprise of life in the Spirit is to make that story one's own," Cathy answered, when I spoke with her at home. "It becomes second nature after a while."

I sensed from her response to my questions about her approach to reading Scripture that I was too focused on creative interpretation and rhetorical use of biblical imagery. I was looking at things as a writer and a critic. She instead stressed how her daily interaction with Scripture opened her mind to the text's manifold possibilities, and it was a habit of reflection that guided her.

"It's as if there is a light underneath," she said, describing her daily prayer. "I see something different every time. What rises is what I need."

Cathy situated her approach historically, explaining how morning prayer was an early Christian practice revived by the Reformation. To this she added the relevance she placed on context for her scriptural interpretation, noting how a particular occasion, social issue, or congregation might affect her perception at any given moment.

I may not pray every day the way Cathy does, but what she described made perfect sense. I noticed how methods of divination that have fascinated me also rely on a repeated contemplation of a text — be it a book, cards, or shells — that "signifies" differently in each encounter. But then I also realized that there is a way in which most forms of textual engagement are indebted to the kind of reflection that is Cathy's daily habit. When you want to know what a text conveys beyond the sum of its words, you have to make it become a part of you through repeated encounters. The richer the material, and the more you immerse yourself in it, the more you will see there.

That embrace of the metaphorical dimension of biblical language and of its infinite interpretive potential directly contradicted the positivist approach of Christian fundamentalism, of which Cathy had recently been publicly critical. She drew a distinction for me between the Bible as inspirational and as inerrant:

"It's a way to say that God is dead. It's a way of saying that we can't act in any way that wasn't prescribed two thousand years ago. So you don't have God in a box, but you have him in a book, and therefore you don't have to encounter ambiguity in your own life."

She went on to criticize fundamentalism for its ethnocentrism and for its lack of sensitivity to historical context, and then she reminded me that years ago I gave her daughter a book of Arab folktales. "That book gave me insight into Middle Eastern thinking and storytelling and into a Middle Eastern approach to language. Nothing could be more wrongheaded than imposing a literalist interpretation!"

I caught myself feeling somewhat surprised to find how intellectually similar our outlooks and approaches were. I could hardly believe that I had so little trouble translating her comments about Scripture and ministry into more familiar analogous scenarios. Cathy's emphasis upon elasticity — be it expansiveness, collaboration, or openness to difference, to adaptation — as key to her vision of what she called life in the Spirit not only made sense, but it squared completely with what I believe is right. The polysemy of the Bible does not diminish its truth — on the contrary, it multiplies it.

The fear of ambiguity Cathy pointed to in fundamentalism was not dissimilar from the fear of change she associated with other traditionalists, even those within her own church. I tried to find a considerate way to ask about what responses there had been to her support of increasingly diverse congregations, wondering how it would eventually affect the older perception of the Episcopalian Church as the province of an aristocratic Anglo elite.

"Traditionalists are afraid that change means losing their identity, but tradition is a living thing. They're afraid that if they change, they might die," she began. "I believe that people on the margins, when brought to the center, lead us into new life," she added.

Then she stood and looked at me with absolute seriousness. In her most forceful preacher's voice she said, "It might not be bad to die. We are, theoretically, the people of the Resurrection. So why should we fear death?" I couldn't think of an answer for her. The bishop had several more meetings that day, so it was time to end our conversation. I mentioned that I hadn't asked her the obvious "but you're a woman" question.

"No, you haven't, but I have an answer for you," she said. She's just so good at this, I thought. It's as if she had been preparing for this moment for her entire life. "I did not strive to become a woman bishop," she avowed. "I want to be a bishop for all people, and I bring my womanness to it.

"But what I was not prepared for," she continued, "was the impact of the iconography on other women. Sometimes, at the Communion rail, as I put the bread into their hands, I can see just a side-glance and a sly smile of recognition." She cupped her hands together and turned her head to the side in imitation of her parishioners. "I'm glad to be able to bear that for women."

With that, the bishop gave me and her husband our good-bye hugs, slipped her cellular phone into her purse, and bustled out the door.

Sermon with Meath

Barry Hannah

MEATH was the teenage son who lived behind us down the hill and across the great meadow. Webb Meath. In our subdivision the well-off and the genteel poor were mixed. Some of the homes were frame houses of WWII vintage and others, like ours and the Meaths', were big, brick, and ranch style, as the Eisenhower years dictated. But there was no snobbery of money in our town in deep Mississippi. Nobody had that much, and across the tracks south of the feed mill, the darker people had nothing.

You could see in the basement quarters through big glass sliding doors the playroom, as they called it, of Webb Meath. Meath was seventeen, and I was only thirteen. I could see him putting 45 rpm records on a machine and practicing dance steps by himself around the playroom. I was going to enter Meath's world fairly soon — bee bop a Lula she's my baby, '59 Pontiac Bonneville, Are You Sincere?, wrist corsages, white socks with black Weejun penny loafers, and such. So I was very watchful of Meath. Meath was struggling, even I knew. He was on the verge of being a sissy, even though he was on the football team, not playing much until all was hopeless or well in hand in the last quarter. Then he would trot in with great earnestness and get some grass stain on his uniform for when he met his girlfriend, who had almost made the cheerleader squad and hung around those girls like an extra pal, no hard feelings. She was almost cute, too. But Meath was built like a soft bowling pin. Although tall, he didn't seem to have any strength to him, and he slouched, with a high burr haircut on him and the red bowed lips of a woman, full and wet like that. Webb Meath was from Indiana or perhaps Minnesota; his folks were fresh in town from alien parts. They were Methodists in a heavily Baptist town, further alien. Webb wanted to be a Methodist preacher. He would bring a Bible out where I and a couple of other buddies my age played at a wideboard rope swing hung from an oak at the bottom of our property, right where the Meath meadow began, out there where we had fierce touch-football games with fellows of all ages.

Meath would stand there with his Bible in hand, more than a foot taller, and watch our play sternly, as if whatever we were doing was not quite right. For instance, plastic soldiers spread all out in attack formation with tanks, artillery, command bunkers, and fortresses of packed soil. We would air-bomb them too, with spark plugs, and fire into them with white-head matches from shooters made of clothespins. Smoke and mouth gunfire and screams going on in grim earnest. Meath would observe us with pity on his face, but kind pity. We all liked Meath. He was gentle like a brother, and he was very strange. Meath would not interrupt; he would let us play ourselves out, then he would hunker down, peer at each of us sincerely, wet his lips, and begin preaching from the Book of Revelation, the Bible spread out in his big left hand. We would sit on our butts with arms around our knees and listen for upwards of an hour.

The Eagle and the Bear and the Horsemen and the White

Horse of Death and the minions and the princes and Joseph Stalin and the Hydrogen Bomb and the Daughters of Wrath. I don't think Meath had a very good grasp of all this, but he listed them well, and in that Northern voice somewhere between a whine and a song. His eyes would half shut as if it hurt to read these things. Many years later it would strike me that those who especially loved Revelation were nerds and dweebs and dorks who despised people and life on this planet, somewhat like the *Star Trek* crowd I saw at Iowa City, who liked to get in elevators and discuss how this or that civilization was "utterly consumed." But I don't believe Meath hated this world. He wanted in it badly but something was very wrong. He was not winning, and he had no joy being regular and mature. He did not dance well, his girl was not so special, he was awkward and had made only second team, and in the school halls he was galootlike, slouching and puzzled as if lost among bad smells. Even we little guys noticed it.

That he had a good car and his people were well-off cut no ice. With another person it might have, but not with Meath. He stayed at the edge of the popular crowd, giving bad imitations of it. For instance, it was difficult for Meath to look casual. He seemed near tears often. I once saw him and his girlfriend having a quiet moment at the hall locker like you were supposed to, but both of them were red faced and pouted up as if nearly crying over some deep matter. It was my sense she wanted him to do things.

After Meath finished the sermon, he would begin playing with us and our soldiers, or whatever we had going, with more zeal by far than he had shown for the sermon. Meath would really get into it, making machine-gun sounds and totally successful bomb explosions. His mouth would be red from wetting the kitchen matches on the heads before striking them. You sailed them and they left true smoke like rockets, bursting into flame as they fell among the soldiers.

Then one afternoon he got very concerned and stared at his hands, and we asked him what was wrong.

They don't think this is right, he said.

Who? What? I asked him.

Me hanging out with guys your age.

Oh. Why not?

It's queer, Dad said.

No. But we need your sermons.

Yes, that's true, said Meath, more confident now. He fell to playing with us again. Meath wasn't just hanging out with us. He was deeper in play than we were.

One other afternoon he said he thought we were mature enough to follow along in Revelation with our own Bibles, so I went up the hill to my house and got several Bibles. We had plenty. My mother was huge in the Baptist Church. She was the president of the state Women's Missionary Union. We had had Mexicans and Chinese people in our house. Where are you going with those? my mother wanted to know. I told her Meath was preaching from Revelation and wanted us to follow. Mother peered down the hill where Meath stood among my other pals. She had that Nay look in her eyes. Baptists are the Church of the New Testament, they say, but in the South they tend to be as severe as in the Old. My mother didn't believe in dancing or too much fun on the Sabbath. I never saw her affectionate with my pa, not once. If the doors of the church were open, we were in it. With revivals, six days a week. She insisted on tithing to such a comprehensive extent that my father complained even to me. He was afraid she would give everything to the church in the event he died, so he lived a good long time. He was from the Depression, when a nickel was serious.

Children shouldn't try to understand that book, she said.

But there's Meath.

Yes. He's a large boy, isn't he. She looked very doubtful as I left with the Bibles. I knew it didn't look right to her, and felt guilty, a common condition of young Baptists. My mother was from Delta planters. Somehow this made her consumed by appearances. The *appearance* of evil was as grave as, say, yelling "hell" at the dinner table, almost.

Then another afternoon, a Sunday, Meath became entirely strange. We were playing touch football. Meath was far and away the largest out there. There must have been sixteen of us from junior high, and Meath, on his perfect, sunlit property. My team did a sweep, and I blocked Meath at the knees. I cut him down. I was shocked that this huge boy went over with only a soft, rubbery give to him. We scored, but we looked back and there was Meath rolling on the ground and howling, holding his shins. It was a thing I could barely connect with my block. I couldn't have weighed more than ninety or so. He was two hundred. But he wailed and then just began clinching up, all red and weepy, going on in an embarrassing thin Yankee whine. It was a preposterous act. We all hung our heads. Soon we went home. All joy was gone, and it made us feel bad. My friends and I began to despise Meath. We watched his failures and cheered for them bitterly.

He and the girl broke up. He prowled around even sadder. We liked this. Some older boy pointed out that Meath had a low ass. This was true, and we adored it. His voice, which we had liked before, got on our nerves. We moved the soldiers back onto my property, abandoning the great forts on his and watching the rains of the spring melt them down. We would jump bikes off a ramp and then leap from the bikes at the peak of the rise, grab a rope that swung out forty feet high into a fir tree, and fall through the branches, usually hurt and even bleeding, which was the point. Meath came down and watched us from his swing. We knew he wanted to join us.

His mouth's connected to his butthole, whispered the older boy.

What?

No guts, the boy explained. This was a rich one, and we barked the rest of the day about it, taking furtive glances at Meath, whose face with its big woman's lips just hung there sissy and wanting, a splendid annoyance to our play. We learned to cut Meath, just cut him, drop our eyes in the halls of the school when he came near. This was a sweet new social skill. High adolescence was going to be a snap.

Meath was ending his senior year that spring. I don't recall how we knew this in the small town, but it was understood that Meath's father was failing in business. His Southern adventure had not worked out. They were moving back North. When I looked down into Meath's playroom, where he still practiced dancing, I saw the gray air of failure all around him. Somebody had caught him wearing a letter jacket he had not earned in the nearby capital city, Jackson, and this was his certain end. You could sink no lower.

In a frame asbestos-siding house on the street that Meath's faced, down just about five houses on the north side, lived a family that was not genteel poor. They were really poor. They were white, of course, and the father, in his forties, was studying to be a grade school teacher at the little Baptist college in our town. He had many children, and it was said they never ate much but cornflakes. He could not support them at whatever he used to do, so now he was educating himself to move up to the position of teacher, but the four years and odd jobs meant even direr straights for his people. Nevertheless, he had them in church every Sunday, heads all watered down with combing, in sorry clothes but clean. He and his entire family were baptized one Wednesday night at prayer meeting, there in the pool under the stained-glass scene of the Jordan River. Everybody cheered him, and my mother became positively tearful about their goodness and conversion. Mother was stern, but she was loving, profoundly, about new church people. I understand the success of the Baptists in converting the South nearly wholesale, through my mother. There is maternal love in their congregations.

But Mr. Tweedy, the poor man, came out of the water on the preacher's arm all choked up and fighting off the water. Here was an adult who feared water. I turned my head and grinned at another hellion down the pew. At Christmas I helped my father deliver boxes of hams and fruit and cheese to the needy. All of the families were black except the Tweedys, nearly on our own street. This was odd. I felt humiliated for them, even though they were most appreciative and showed no false pride. I knew this was biblical, but it didn't sit right. I recall, also, the absense of damned near everything in the living room of that house. I believe there was a card table and orange crates.

So Mr. Tweedy was graduating too. This spring he was getting his degree and already he was a substitute teacher in Jackson. Things were looking up. Mother and the neighbors cheered them. Providence, it seemed, was about to attend the new Christian Tweedys. Nothing could be better. The Lord had promised this.

But in April, while Mr. Tweedy was driving his awful Ford to his school, a tornado came through Jackson, picked up only his car into the air, and hurled him against something, and killed him. All his plans and work meant this, and his children were now orphans, his skinny, bent wife a widow by celestial violence. I could not understand it at all. Although I played constantly at war with my pals, I could never, I thought, have devised anything this cruel. My mother was hurt too. But she said it had a purpose. All had a design.

But I stopped going to church, scandalizing her and driving her into long prayer talks with our pastor. She went around teary and solemn. My father told me the same thing as when my terrier Spot died of jaundice: Son, everything dies. He could not know how viciously irrelevant he was then. I started growing up cynical. I believe, in the matter of Christians, I became a little Saul before the road to Tarsus, Saul the persecutor of the faith, before he saw the light and became Saint Paul of the Epistles.

My mother came in my room and told me Meath had called me and several of the boys to meet him down at the swing. He had a special testimony for us. I could not believe she was approving of Meath. She was truly desperate. I went down, though sourly, already despising Meath as he stood tall among some boys who had already arrived. Nobody sat down. That was all over. We just sort of made a rank and stepped back from Meath. He had no Bible, but he clasped his hands together and was looking at the ground prayerfully.

What's giving, Reverend, said the older boy.

We're all confused by what happened to Mr. Tweedy, I know, said Meath. He was meek and humble, a hardworking Christian man, a resurrected man, who loved his wife and children. The meek should inherit the earth, the Savior said. But . . . Tweedy.

When Meath raised his face, there was one of those warm evangelical smiles on him. He had let his hair grow out, and it was swept back, all oily, and looked like black under shellac. I hadn't seen him lately, and this was almost too much.

God has his reasons for poor Mr. Tweedy. He was using him as a testament to us. Mr. Tweedy is happy now.

Meath seemed to be imitating Tweedy in heaven with this insane warm smile.

Tweedy is looking down telling us guys to just love and support one another and get right with the Lord!

There was a big gap of quiet then, and many of us looked down at the soil too. Where the forts had been was only a dry mud. That was what God did to Mr. Tweedy, I recall thinking. Right back into the mud for daring to get better.

You only like Tweedy because he's lower than you, the older boy suddenly said to Meath. You love it that he was murdered by a tornado because it makes a creep like you feel lucky and right. You're using Tweedy to make us be your friends. But we ain't going to be your friends, because you're chicken and a liar and that's the way it's always going to be.

I was astounded by what my friend said. He had really been winding up inside in his hatred for Meath, and I was shocked that I hated Meath almost this much too. I had depended on Meath to be smooth and Northern-hip and a friendly guide to life.

Meath's warm new smile fell off and he just collapsed. He turned around and walked back to his two-story house with its glassed playroom. We could see him shaking with sobs. His mother was on the balcony waiting and watching him. We saw the sudden expression on her face, horror, and we left, to all parts of the subdivision. I felt a part of a mob that had stoned somebody, and it was not that bad, it had a nice edge to it. That big Meath.

In college my roommate, a brilliant boy already long into

botany and Freud, and I baited Christers at the college. Many of them were preministerial students perfecting their future roles. They came on like idiot savants, quoting Scripture perfectly and at great length but baffled by almost everything else. We especially went at a short boy with a wide, pale face and thick, ashy whiskers on him. He wore thick glasses and was a quoting fool, get him started. He was only eighteen but already like a loony old man. He roomed with a New Christian Chinese fellow, rail thin and just out of starvation, who wrote this hesitant Christian poetry on the slant for the campus literary magazine. It was utter banal coonshit, and we loved to read it aloud. We played loud Ray Charles and much jazz on the machine, smoked, and drank lab alcohol, and shouted out what we would do if challenged by one of the nude pinup girls on our walls. The Christers gathered and put us on all the prayer lists. The dorm counselor, a one-eyed giant Christer, broke down and told us nothing came from our room but crap and corruption. But we made A's, anointed thus. Once I hid in the closet while my buddy pretended to be in a spiritual crisis, weeping and gnashing his teeth, for the loony thick-glassed guy, who was overjoyed at his chance to save him. I finally howled out. The boy was so out of it, he thought I was in a fit of contrition too. Then I went down and pretended to the Christian Chinese boy that his poetry had driven me insane.

I am not proud remembering this. Once I thrashed a skinny Christer, a senior, with boxing gloves in the hall. He had been wanting to prove that Christians were strong too, but I routed him. I was cheered by the agnostic few around the hall, but this seemed cheap, at last, and I gave up open baiting. My roommate-pal went straight to the state asylum for depression and alcoholism, and I felt so miserable and lonely I got married too early.

A couple of decades passed, and I was in Chicago, reading

some pages from my new book at the university, I think, when I saw something in the paper. That night I got a taxi and went out to see him. Meath was indeed a minister, Methodist, but in a small sort of hippie chapel on the edge of a garish bad neighborhood where transvestites sported around nearly in ownership of the block. Meath was overjoyed to see me. He met me an hour before the service began, and although I had come wanting vaguely to apologize for our awful treatment of him twenty years ago, I never got the chance. He hugged me and acted as if we had been perfect boyhood chums. He bragged on good traits about me I didn't even remember, said he knew my imagination would pull me through. He too had been through divorce and bad times, although always a minister. He was stout, not much hair, but trimmer, more solid, and glowing with health. Mostly he was so happy to see me.

At the service were some forty folks — some bums, some straight and prosperous men and women, and some truly ancient hippies, those phenomenal people who are fifty and have changed nothing. Meath began as if just chatting, then I sensed the sermon was in progress. He stood, no lectern, no altar, no height, in front of his flock, and spoke with a sane joy. Simply a good-looking middle-aged man with a comfortable interior to him. He wore glasses. A loose hair sprang up at the back of his head and waved about. Everything counts, he said.

Everything counts, but you must isolate this thing and not let it become mixed with others. You must look at it as a child would. You must not bring the heaviness of long thinking and the burden of your hours to it. The lightness, the calm wonder and intensity of a child is what I mean. Picasso said at fifty, At last, I can paint like a child! That must have been paradise for him. Perhaps it waits for you.

Come unto me, all you that labor and are heavy laden, and I will give you rest. Take my yoke upon you and learn of me; for I am meek and lowly in heart. And you shall find rest unto your souls. For my yoke is easy, and my burden is light, speaks Christ.

Heaviness comes as you get older. But sufficient unto the day is the evil thereof, says the Savior. Look at the day alone and do not mix it with others. A child has no need of the future or the past. He is all times at once. You've only need of the day. The precious day. This day even more precious because my friend of long ago is here.

Meath pointed to me.

I can't remember, in my life so far, a happier time than this.

Forthwith

April Bernard

And they came over unto the other side of the sea, into the country of the Gadarenes.

And when he was come out of the ship, immediately there met him out of the tombs a man with an unclean spirit.

Who had his dwelling among the tombs; and no man could bind him, no, not with chains:

Because that he had been often bound with fetters and chains, and the chains had been plucked asunder by him, and the fetters broken in pieces: neither could any man tame him.

And always, night and day, he was in the mountains, and in the tombs, crying, and cutting himself with stones.

But when he saw Jesus afar off, he ran and worshipped him,

And cried with a loud voice, and said, What have I to do with thee, Jesus, thou Son of the most high God? I adjure thee by God, that thou torment me not.

For he said unto him, Come out of the man, thou unclean spirit.

And he asked him, What is thy name? And he answered, saying, My name is Legion: for we are many.

And he besought him much, that he would not send them away out of the country.

Now there was there, nigh unto the mountains, a great herd of swine feeding.

And all the devils besought him, saying, Send us into the swine, that we may enter into them.

And forthwith Jesus gave them leave. And the unclean spirits went out, and entered into the swine; and the herd ran violently down a steep place into the sea, (they were about two thousand,) and they were choked in the sea.

And they that fed the swine fled, and told it in the city, and in the country. And they went out to see what it was that was done.

And they come to Jesus, and see him that was possessed with the devil, and had the legion, sitting, and clothed, and in his right mind: and they were afraid.

MARK 5:1–15

CRYING AND CUTTING

Mark has a narrative knack for clear action touched by pathos, often as cartoon corny as a John Ford Western — here, however, the strangeness of the story overpowers the usual attempt to draw a clear moral. (Apart from the moral throughout; that Jesus can *do* anything.) Sequence is screwed up; "he" at any point can be Jesus, the possessed demoniac, the devil. Who says what? How many are a legion? A Roman legion was six thousand men, but Mark breathlessly tells us, midstory, that there are two thousand devils, or swine, or both. A herd of two thousand swine? Maybe not a full legion, but a lot of pigs. The devils don't want to leave home, their country. The pigs run over a cliff into the sea. Some witnessed, others heard the story: and they were afraid.

This story hardens on me like glue. It will not wash away.

Stones are the first weapons of choice the world over, although in the lands called the cradle of civilization they have a peculiar local power. No doubt this is because there are so many stones lying around. The Palestinians throw rocks at Israeli soldiers who are armed with guns. Farther east, in Afghanistan, the newly dominant Islamic regime has reinstituted stoning as the punishment for adultery. A newspaper account tells of the public ceremony of a man and woman buried up to their necks in the dirt, then to have their bare heads stoned by the men of the town. The stoning stops when the culprits are declared dead, which can take longer than you might think; more than an hour for that particular man, I believe it was.

In New England, another land of stony soil, witches were pressed to death by stones piled on boards, a sort of instrument of execution and coffin in one. This was also a public ceremony, like the more commonplace hanging, to which you could bring the children, and refreshments. Once a devil had taken possession, the only way to eliminate it was to eliminate its human host.

I have visited mental wards of state hospitals, in New England and elsewhere in America, where even the spoons are plastic, lest the patients cut themselves. Of course, knives, forks, belts, jewelry, stones have been removed. Things are much the same in prisons. And in both institutions, the inmates are dressed in forms of pajamas, like a swaddling or a shroud.

He was crying and cutting himself with stones. There's a fetish phenomenon described by psychologists as "delicate self-cutting." Almost always, this is a female disorder; hence, perhaps, the delicacy. With any number of instruments — razors, scissors, small sharp delicate stones — the woman will repeatedly cut the same area on her body: bleeding, scabbing, scraping the scab, scarring, cutting the scar, never healing. The area might be her scalp, hidden beneath her hair; the inside of her elbow, beneath her sleeve; a special place on her shod foot. The power of the wound inheres in its secrecy, its delicacy; as private stigmata, the left arm not knowing that the right arm is bleeding.

Surely we also know the grander gestures: the man who slams himself into the wall, the pistol in the mouth, the hara-kiri sword to the abdomen, the woman who throws herself from the seventeenth floor and breaks on the stones of the courtyard below.

But here in Mark's story, we have an indelicate self-cutter, openly self-punishing though not self-destroying. The devil who inhabits him keeps him alive and in misery. Indeed, that this man lives among the tombs is a terrible taunt: he dwells restless, wounded, among the restful dead. He cannot rest even in chains; his devil's strength is such that he breaks his human chains, the better to writhe under the shackles of his spirit.

Of course Jesus does not torment him further; instead, he goes right to the point and asks not the man's, but the devil's, name.

And the devil replies: "My name is Legion: for we are many."

LEGION

How interesting, within the mono-theistic edifice of the Bible, wherein God most famously names himself "I Am," that the devil finds himself numerous. He is many. They are many. I am many. We are many.

How imposing is a legion? Six thousand Roman soldiers, hel-meted and spear-carrying, advance in rows across a plain. Unfor-tunately, given our cultural referents, this picture is daubed in garish Technicolor, and some strong-jawed ham from the 1950s marches in the front row; therefore this does not frighten as it might. Let us instead think of the legion as a swarm. If we must have the movies, and we must, think of Kurosawa's warrior swarms.

Think of a swarm of white maggots busily churning about in a dead crow you have just turned over with the toe of your boot.

It is not easy to look with complacency at the activity of a beehive, even when the bees are encased safely behind glass. No one loved the rats of Hamelin. There is something terrible about a swarm, the apparently disorganized but desperately motivated movement, the way the individual ant or rat or maggot or refugee has its own vibrating life as it is carried along in the wave of collective purpose.

Let me not be unclear: humans in the mass alarm and disgust as well, in their swarms. The power of a crowd, when one is in it, can be exhilarating; but too much shoving nudges that spot in the hindbrain that warns, that says No as clearly as the snake's hiss. As for the crowd that one is not in, the mob of strangers observed from a height — say, as the plane dips low over the Ganges, over the favelas of Rio, over the Cairo bazaar — the people look "like ants," we exclaim, meaning like pests, like something that should be crushed by a great big foot.

And what about a swarm of swine? Biologically as well as morally, pigs are a lot like humans; the parallel has escaped few cultures. When Circe turned her suitors into swine, she was performing a familiar act of caricature. George Orwell merely took the insult to its logical conclusion: "You pig." And cannibals have reported that human flesh does not taste "like chicken," but rather, "like pork." Therefore the request made to Jesus by the devils to leave the man and inhabit the herd of swine grazing nearby came from no great imaginative leap. Six thousand of one, half a dozen thousand of the other.

So we know that the malevolence of six thousand, or perhaps

only two thousand, pigs had been inhabiting this one poor man. When he opened his mouth, the voice of the pig legion spoke. And they did not want to leave that country; they were happy there. Don't send us from our home; don't send us into exile; we wouldn't want to be refugees. And forthwith — as Jesus does so many things in Mark's account — he gives them leave.

THE JOKE

One of the oldest parables of overpopulation is that of the lemmings, who eat and mate and eat and mate until there are too many of them. They have eaten every insect for miles, famine is upon them, and one, no doubt in a (for a rodent) strong-jawed gesture, leads the way for the legions of fellow lemmings to leap to their deaths in the sea.

When Jesus gave the devils leave to inhabit the swine, we must assume he knew that this too would engender a sort of population crisis; two thousand pigs is one thing, but two thousand pigs plus a legion of devils is another. Jesus does not usually cut an especially antic figure; nevertheless, this is one of his rare jokes, a practical joke at that: You want to stay in the country? Fine, go ahead. Surprise! You drown.

The devils "besought him much" that he would not send them away. They pleaded with him; they acknowledged his power. They asked for his mercy. And yet he sent them running, "violently," into the sea to choke and drown in the salt water.

Violently the devil-pigs run, just as violently the devil-man had cut himself with stones. Violence is the devil's trademark, and here Jesus has unleashed it to its logical conclusion, of self-destruction. Interestingly, Mark does not explicitly tell us of Jesus' agency in the matter — the charge of the swine into the sea just happens once Jesus has given the devils leave. Perhaps that's part of Jesus' sense of humor: Who, me?

ACTION AS PARABLE

I don't think we can really understand this story unless we read it in context. In the Gospel of Mark, this tale of the demoniac and the swine follows the crucial account of Jesus telling the parable of the sower.

I will simplify: The sower casts his seed onto hard, stony ground; and he casts it among the thorns; and he casts it on fertile ground. The seed on the stony ground never takes root; the seed among the thorns takes root, but then is choked out by the thorns; only the seed that falls upon fertile ground will take root and thrive. So, Jesus adds, it is with you.

The disciples, puzzled, ask Jesus why he preaches to the crowd in parables. And Jesus answers, memorably, horribly: So that seeing they will not see, and hearing they will not understand.

The disciples press for further explanation, and Jesus says that the word of God is like the seed that the sower casts — it can only grown upon fertile ground. If it falls on stone-deaf ears, or into thorny hearts, it cannot prosper.

In other words, you either get it or you don't.

He has, in fact, explained his parable — though only to his disciples — which he claims to have told as parable to the crowd because he would not explain it.

In other words, you cannot be taught the word of God; you can only recognize it.

And you can only recognize that which you already know.

Not too much later, we are told our story of the demoniac and the swine and the devils who fall into the sea. Thus this miracle itself, Jesus' action, functions as parable.

And you either get it or you don't.

AFRAID

The phrase "And they were afraid" is reiterated throughout the Gospels. The witnesses to Jesus' glory were constantly being made afraid by his power to disrupt the natural order. The shepherds in the field who saw the star over Bethlehem, the eaters of the loaves and fishes, those who saw Lazarus raised from the dead and the lame made to walk and the blind made to see, the disciples in the boat when Jesus walked on water, all were afraid, and some of them were even sore afraid.

Here again the witnesses are afraid. They see the demoniac, the famous madman, restored. He is "in his right mind," and no longer naked or in tatters, no longer helpless, but properly clothed. What, after all, could be more terrifying than someone who is sane?

I am afraid of this parable; I am afraid of its rhetorical power; I am afraid that its power is not merely rhetorical; I am afraid of the word made flesh; I am afraid of Jesus.

Like all sinners, I am multiple, and I lead multiple lives. Sometimes I foolishly congratulate myself on my breadth: look, I can write alexandrines, cook osso buco, sink the six ball in the side pocket, dance the merengue, hang the washing, listen to your problems, identify the Bach invention, cite chapter and verse. More often, I am in a haze of miserable self-accusation: because I cannot concentrate, I cannot do any one thing truly well. And this does not begin to address the multiplicity made possible by even the most rudimentary use of technology in telephones, computers, CDs, and cars. Although I complain about it, I have always chosen to be in more than one place at once — teaching here, living there, visiting for the weekend, traveling for the month, also living *there,* subletting back home, planning to go somewhere else, and meanwhile talking on the phone to everyone everywhere. Traditional nomadism, in its stately, epic movements according to the seasons, seems staid by comparison with this frantic, petty agitation.

When of so many places, so many minds, how could one ever be in one's "right" mind? I am mad, and sinful, in my multiplicity. Indeed, I have been known to cry, and also to cut myself with stones. Fetters have not held me — and I have knocked aside the loving hands that would restrain me. In the face of those who would cure me, I have grown stubborn and clung to my troubles. These are mine; do not send them away.

This story promises me that I will remain a demoniac, aswarm, as long as I resist the singular sanity, the right-mindedness, of Christianity. I knew that already; I have seen, and understood; I got it long ago. But just as I resist the sanity of atheism, I resist the sanity of belief. Doubting, mad, my name is Legion: for we are many.

Afterword
The Baby

Darcey Steinke

Jesus saw some infants nursing. He said to his disciples. "These infants are like those who enter the kingdom of heaven." They said to him, "How then can we enter?" Jesus said to them, "When you make the two one, and when you make the inside like the outside, and the outside like the inside, and the upper like the lower and when you make male and female into a single one, then you will enter the kingdom."

THE GOSPEL OF THOMAS

I

When I was four, my brother was born, came home briefly, developed pneumonia, and had to be rushed back to the hospital — where the pediatric nurses fed him liquid orange Jell-O in a room thick with vaporizer steam. A few days later, the doctor called in the middle of the night to say that the baby might die, so we loaded into our station wagon and drove to the hospital. My father, using Styrofoam cups from the corridor by the nurses' station, baptized the tiny red baby that lay limp and glassy eyed in my mother's arms. My mother, her raincoat thrown over her nightgown, cried inconsolably, while my father, in his black preacher pants and yesterday's undershirt, tried to control his shaking hands.

My mother stayed at the hospital to hold the baby. On the way home, my father, who usually drove casually, his wrist flung over the wheel, clenched the steering wheel with both hands and leaned forward, glancing up out of the top of the windshield as if searching the sky for the tiny soul of a baby.

I was upset that my parents were so discombobulated; they seemed to have forgotten about me. I knew that we'd baptized the baby so that he'd be allowed into heaven, but I wasn't sure if they took babies there. Were the angels willing to change diapers and warm up bottles of formula? It was a good time to clarify some of my more pressing religious questions.

"Is your soul near your heart?" I asked in the car. My father smiled that smile that meant you'd said something naive, even goofy. He didn't answer. Maybe he assumed I already knew about the nature of the soul and was just making small talk. While my mother was pregnant I was often accused of asking questions to which I already knew the answer in an effort to seem babyish and cute.

"Or is it by your lungs?"

He glanced at me. "Your soul isn't like your heart or your lungs," he said. "It's invisible."

I'd always assumed that my soul, while maybe a notch above, was just one more fleshy organ, less like slimy refrigerator leftovers, more like the elegant angel fish in the dentist's office fish tank. I thought of things invisible — air, breath, wind, germs — but none of these seemed substantial enough to represent a person.

"Like a ghost?" I was familiar, for example, with Casper.

"Not exactly." He shook his head and lapsed again into silence, his eyes watching the wet road. In the rush to the hospital, he'd forgotten his coat and his arms were goose-pimpled, pale and thin as my own.

My father's vulnerability connected somehow to the mysterious nature of the soul, and I kept wondering, given this new information, what this essence might look like. I'd once seen a cartoon of a doughnut with wings hovering over a coffin. A girl in Sunday school had told me the soul looked like a dove. But neither of these seemed plausible now. "So it sort of floats around inside you?"

"You could say that," he answered without conviction, as if it were bad luck to talk about this now. The silence in the car muscled up then. I was an expert at judging the malleability and meaning of silence, but this one solidified and became impenetrable. I couldn't think of anything monumental or clever enough with which to break into it, so I started saying my nighttime prayers to myself. *Now I lay me down to sleep; I pray the Lord my soul to keep,* and so forth. Then I listed all the things I wanted: from the sick baby to live all the way down to the Fisher Price cash register, when the list ran into silliness. I wanted animals to talk, and grass to be lime-flavored candy. I remember it started to rain hard; I watched the windshield wipers swing back and forth until they hypnotized me, and the heat got so warm I fell asleep.

My mother stayed at the hospital all day and into the night. It was the first time I'd been away from her, and I missed her desperately, in the same visceral way one misses a lover. I wanted to smell her and touch her collarbone and put my palm to her cheek. I cried as my father put me to bed and we said a prayer for the sick baby. When he left the room I decided to stay awake all night. I was still young enough to believe my actions magically

239

affected everything, and I figured if I could stay up, keep vigil, the baby might live.

So I listened to the radiators shudder and watched the tiny silent airplanes swim across the black horizon. After a while I got so tired I lapsed into a waking dream. I was in the dark cry room at the back of the church, arm babies fretting on exhausted mother's shoulders, lap babies drooling on their knees. My father's service was broadcast there through a tiny speaker set up high in a corner. I walked to the front of the little room, watching through thick soundproof glass, as my father, blond and thin as any angel, moved around the altar, the lilies brushing the cuff of his robe, the silver chalice bright as a fragment of the sun. In my little-girl consciousness, I'd already divided the world into good places and bad places, into heavens and hells. Heaven was the shady side of the house where the white violets grew, where I'd once seen a butterfly move inside a cocoon; hell the loft of the run-down barn adjacent to the house, where dead birds lay in sprawling heaps on top of bound newspapers. Heaven was my parents' bed, hell the garbage can under the kitchen sink. The altar, with the mysterious eternal flame and the white flowers, was the surest and most sacred of heavens, and the cry room, which reeked of spit-up and was littered with broken toys, dirty stuffed animals, and moaning babies, was the entrance into hell.

Later that night I heard a flutter on the other side of my room, the same delicate flapping a sparrow makes on taking off from a tree branch. There was an angel hovering in the corner. She looked just like Miss Truelove, my beloved nursery school teacher, and she told me in her sweet, benevolent voice, before she faded like twilight, that the baby would be all right.

My first impulse was to run downstairs to where my father was drinking coffee and reading the newspaper beside the telephone to tell him that an angel told me the baby was getting better. But I remembered how he'd mocked Mrs. Claytor after she told him about the stone Jesus lifting up its marble arms. And also how he'd scoffed at Mr. Mulhoffer, who told everybody that if it wasn't for the Virgin Mary coming to him, he'd never have been able to quit drinking. Already I knew Lutheranism was somber and that my father held great disdain for Catholic exuberance and Pentecostal hysteria.

In the morning I found out what I already knew; the baby would live. He and my mother came home a few days later, and I was disappointed my little brother couldn't talk, walk, or do much of anything. I was confused as to why the little zombie so persistently held my mother's attention. But her preoccupation was okay, because I had other things on my mind. Though it was the baby that nearly died, I was the one that had changed completely. Obsessed now with the spirit world.

Imaginary friends crowded into my room, poised on the edge of the bed or troll-like next to my globe upon the bookshelf. I began to talk to them so incessantly that my parents worried I was showing early signs of schizophrenia. I remember now only the empathetic white horse named Cheerio and a morose little boy in a gray wool jumper whom I called Harold. I overheard my father tell my mother how a boy from church was so anxious to see heaven that he kept trying to ride his Big Wheel off the garage roof. This seemed to me a reasonable solution to my own uncertainties, and I decided to follow suit. I'd drown myself in the bathtub or jump out my bedroom window. I'd put my finger into the electrical socket, something I'd been warned against for years. I refined the details of these various plans until they took on a life of their own and began to haunt me. I became obsessed with funerals. Were there breathing holes in coffins? What did it really feel like to be dead? Supernatural monsters frightened me more than Stranger Danger. Even at four I'd figured out that if angels made appearances then devils existed too. So I kept a baton underneath my pillow and garlic on the window ledge. I got it in my head that the Bible sent swarms of locusts to punish children who touched the glass vase on the coffee table or broke the eggs in the refrigerator. These domestic sins I was successful in curbing, but what about lying and exaggeration? Try as I might, I could never seem to control these compulsions, and so at night I'd lie in bed listening for the demons to come through the windows to claim me as their own. Sometimes I'd become so terrified I was certain my heart would stop beating, and I'd calm myself by conjuring up kittens or strawberries or my mother's beautiful face.

This period came to an end one Halloween. My room had just been painted and so I was sleeping on a cot at the end of the hallway as not to inhale any of the paint fumes. These fumes I envisioned as tendrils of poisonous gas unfurling down the darkened hallway. Watching the sky for flying witches, I listened too, figuring in this day and age they probably rode vacuum cleaners instead of brooms.

Sometime during the night, wind slapped tree branches against the window, and I looked up and saw a cat covered with lizard skin perched in the pear tree. Its grotesque little face peeked out from behind red and yellow leaves. I ran, terrified, into my parents' room, snuggled in by my mother's side, and slept fitfully, waking occasionally to the sinister lump hung over the open closet door like a corpse. It wasn't until the light at the window turned from black to gray that I made out my father's black minister pants and shirt, his white clerical collar looking alternately like a halo and a dog's leash.

11

At the onset of Advent, my baby brother started sleeping through the night, and I was no longer startled awake every few hours by his fiendish cries. The household returned to its former order, my mother was more available to me, and I began to get over my maudlinness and to prepare for the arrival of Christmas and the baby Jesus.

I found this celebration, as I did each year in our clerical household, a great relief. Rather than thinking about the strange Jesus who went around barefoot saying confusing things about a camel going through the eye of a needle or that your mother wasn't really your mother, or worse, the spooky, half-dead Jesus hanging from the cross, I could meditate on a tiny infant, no bigger than one of my dolls.

I loved that I was older than baby Jesus and so could have some authority over him. This feeling of mastery helped me to regain my composure and dissolve my attachment to the dark side. Sometimes I'd pretend my little brother was baby Jesus and creep into his room at night to see if he radiated light, but his only magic was a toothless smile that sent both my parents into a state of euphoria. At the same time, I had been trying to put the cat into a trance and to get the rabbits in the yard to come up to me: I was also impressed that baby Jesus had induced animals to stand quietly and watch him sleep. Sheep, horses, those fascinating and exotic two-humped camels. Above all else, this convinced me that the baby was in possession of the godhead.

The Christmas before, much to my dismay, my doll Kimmie had played the part of baby Jesus in the children's nativity. *Kimmie is a girl,* I remember thinking indignantly as I sat with my mother in the front row and watched the dark-haired Mary pick up my doll and show her reverently to Joseph. But finally I'd come to realize that it was an honor, as my father was always insisting, for my doll to play the little Lord. So as we lit the purple candles in the pine-needle wreath and opened the little cardboard windows of the Advent calendar, I began to give Kimmie baby Jesus lessons. I taught her how to look like a boy, how to say "Mary" and "Joseph," and how not to cry when the angels came down. Efforts to get her to sing "Silent Night," however, and to glow in the dark, were unsuccessful. Mostly, baby Jesus was sort of lazy. Just like my little brother, all she wanted to do was sleep in my toy cradle nestled in the crumpled paper I'd colored yellow to look like straw.

When the big night came, I stood in the pulpit wrapped in a bedsheet gown, cardboard wings covered in tinfoil attached to my back and a clothes-hanger halo, looking down into a manger filled with real straw. I saw Kimmie's natty blond bangs. Just that morning I'd sheared the synthetic threads off with scissors so everyone could see the blue lines I'd drawn with Magic Marker round her eyes.

My father read the Christmas story from Luke, and while the congregation sang "What Child Is This," I tried to figure out what it might be like to have a baby, and what could be inside the baby brain of God. This was to be my first epiphany, for as I tried to get my thoughts around the hurricane-velocity winds, the zillion particles of light, the unfathomable swirl that I thought of (even then) as the life force, I felt time wobble sideways and got so dizzy, looking down into the manger, that I had to lean against the rail of the pulpit for support.

III

Birth makes nearly everyone uncomfortable. When I was a little girl, the contemplation of the creative force almost overwhelmed me, and later, when I was actually pregnant, a fretful anticipation permeated the last weeks of waiting. Then there's the anxiety birth can cause in childless adults. During my pregnancy I was amazed how many close female friends devalued the birth process. Even ministers stay away from the physicality of Christ's birth in their Christmas morning sermons, spending their twenty minutes either condemning the secular world of Santa or speaking about the infant as if he were the adult Jesus in doll size, an interpretation common to many paintings of Madonna and Child. Whether it's an uneasiness over our physical connection to our mothers or the idea of our own preexistence, birth, much like death, raises the hair on the backs of our collective necks.

So it didn't surprise me, as I recently reread the Nativity scene, that neither Luke nor Matthew gave us the details of Mary's labor. Though both should have known that labors make great narratives. Refined with multiple telling, they remain, even today, a vital part of our oral tradition. And why is Jesus' blood fetishized later at the Crucifixion, while the Nativity is rendered neat and clean as a Christmas card? Maybe Luke, after placing Mary in the barn, couldn't bring himself to portray her pain? And baby Jesus? While the Bible specifies nothing of his temperament, folklore and Christmas carols portray him as the perfect infant, meek and mild.

This sanitation disturbs me, for what we miss if we discount the pain of Mary's labor and the babyness, the complete human helplessness, of baby Jesus is that — as in the Crucifixion — Jesus is at his most powerful when he is completely vulnerable. Besides, birth and death are connected. These events bookend each life, and it's natural that some of the same elements reside in our first moments and our last.

Most biblical scholars agree that accounts of Jesus' birth are apocryphal, myths conjured up to further the themes of Jesus' work. That Mary's first visitors were shepherds and Jesus' birthplace a barn are writerly manifestations of the New Testament message of inclusiveness and resistance to material wealth. Still, it's hard not to insert oneself into the Nativity scene. As a child dressed as an angel, I watched from the pulpit, and now that I've had a baby, I can't help identifying with Mary. Well, the challenge of the religious life is to make the Bible stories singular, to connect with the text, to intertwine and attach the stories to a mythology of one's own.

So in this spirit, let me give you a sense of Mary's labor. She probably paced the barn, as women did before the scientific model of sickness led doctors to urge them onto their backs. Cool dirt darkened the soles of her bare feet. Cows and sheep, troubled by her moaning, shifted uneasily in their pens. Pain, which until this night meant to her a more contained and minor thing, is so different in form and texture now, so persuasive she seems to be drowning in it. The pain washes away all pretense, wears away identity, renders Mary penetrable, the air, the light, the music from the inn, all moving through her until she's the same as the barn's walls, the lowing animals. The aura from a candle looks golden and mealy as a hallucination, and through a rent in the wood she sees the blue black night, oozing in like oil, inking the hem of her robe. Blood mixed with amniotic fluid and scented like seaweed runs down her legs as she squats, steadies herself on

Joseph's shoulder, grits her teeth, and bears down. Feels her pelvis opening, her consciousness, as if made of paper, ripping in two, a sensation so painful, powerful, and disorienting that she senses as the crown of the baby's head appears, matted with black hair, that a radical transformation is already in the works. And it's in this last delirious moment, as the Bible so succinctly puts it, that Mary brings forth her firstborn son.

But before she wraps him in swaddling clothes, before she lays him in the manger, before this book ends where it all begins for baby Jesus and for each of us, let's allow Mary to hold him against her chest. Let her feel the exquisite touch of his delicate fingertips as the baby shifts his tiny head, mesmerized already by the cadence of her human heart.

Notes on Contributors

MADISON SMARTT BELL is the author of nine novels, including *The Washington Square Ensemble* (1983), *Waiting for the End of the World* (1985), *Straight Cut* (1986), *The Year of Silence* (1987), *Doctor Sleep* (1991), *Save Me, Joe Louis* (1993), and *Soldier's Joy*, which received the Lillian Smith Award in 1989. Bell has also published two collections of short stories: *Zero db* (1987) and *Barking Man* (1990). His eighth novel, *All Soul's Rising*, was a finalist for the 1995 National Book Award and the 1996 PEN/Faulkner Award. His ninth, *Ten Indians*, was published by Pantheon in November 1997.

APRIL BERNARD is the author of two books of poems, *Blackbird Bye Bye* and *Psalms*, and a novel, *Pirate Jenny*. Her essays have appeared in the *New York Review of Books*, *The Nation*, *The New Republic*, *Parnassus*, and *Newsday*.

CATHERINE BOWMAN is the author of two collections of poems, *1-800-HOT RIBS* and *Rock Farm*. She is currently teaching at Indiana University.

JOSEPH CALDWELL is a novelist and playwright. Among his works are *In Such Dark Places*, *The Uncle from Rome*, *Under the Dog Star*, and *The Deer at the River*. He is the recipient of a Rome Prize from the American Academy of Arts and Letters.

BENJAMIN CHEEVER is the author of two novels, *The Plagiarist* and *The Partisan,* and the editor of *The Letters of John Cheever.* He has published in *The New Yorker,* the *New York Times, The Nation,* and numerous other publications. He is currently completing a book of nonfiction for the Free Press as well as a novel. The variety of his endeavors may help to explain why his chapel is not in his mind.

LYDIA DAVIS is the author of *Break It Down, The End of the Story,* and most recently *Almost No Memory,* a collection of stories. She is also the translator of Maurice Blanchot and Michel Leiris, and is currently working on a new version of Proust's *Du Côté de chez Swann.*

JEFFREY EUGENIDES is the author of the novel *The Virgin Suicides.* His fiction has appeared in *The New Yorker,* the *Paris Review,* the *Yale Review,* and *Granta.*

EURYDICE's novel, *f/32,* was published by Fiction Collective Two. She has taught creative writing at Brown University. Her stories and nonfiction have been published widely. She's a staff writer at *Spin* magazine.

COCO FUSCO is a New York–based interdisciplinary artist and writer. She is the author of *English Is Broken Here: Notes on Cultural Fusion in the Americas.*

LUCY GREALY is a poet, essayist, and memoirist. Her work has appeared widely. Her most recent book is *The Autobiography of a Face.*

BARRY HANNAH is the author of ten books. His most recent book of stories, *High Lonesome,* was published by Atlantic Monthly Press in 1996.

BELL HOOKS, a writer and cultural critic, is Distinguished Professor of English at City College in New York. She is the author of many books, most recently *Killing Rage: Ending Racism, Reel to Real: Race, Sex and Class at the Movies,* and two memoirs, *Bone Black: Memories of Girlhood* and *Wounds of Passion: A Writing Life.*

JIM LEWIS is the author of two novels, *Sister* and *Why the Tree Loves the Ax,* and is currently at work on a third.

RICK MOODY is the author of the novels *Garden State, The Ice Storm,* and *Purple America,* and a collection of stories, *The Ring of Brightest Angels Around Heaven.*

ANN PATCHETT is the author of three novels, *The Patron Saint of Liars, Taft,* and *The Magician's Assistant.* She is the recipient of a Guggenheim fellowship and was a Bunting fellow at Radcliffe.

ANN POWERS is writing a personal history of bohemianism in the eighties and nineties to be published by Simon and Schuster. She is the coeditor of *Rock She Wrote: Women Write about Rock, Pop, and Soul.* She has written for the *Village Voice, Spin, Rolling Stone,* the *New York Times,* and other publications.

JOANNA SCOTT is the author of four novels, including *Arrogance* and *The Manikin,* and a collection of short stories, *Various Antidotes.* She is a professor of English at the University of Rochester.

LISA SHEA is the author of the novel *Hula* and is at work on a new novel, *The Free World,* and a book of poetry, *The Thief of Strawberries.* She is the recipient of a Whiting Writer's Award and a New Voice Poetry Award.

DARCEY STEINKE is the author of three novels, *Up Through the Water, Suicide Blonde,* and *Jesus Saves.* She is a contributing editor at *Spin* magazine.

STEPHEN WESTFALL is an artist and writer living in New York City. His essays have appeared in *Art in America, Arts,* and elsewhere. His paintings are represented by Andre Emmerich Gallery. He teaches at the School of Visual Arts and at Bard College.

KIM WOZENCRAFT is the author of the novels *Rush* and *Notes from the Country Club.* She was executive editor of *Prison Life* magazine. Her third novel, *The Catch,* will be published by Doubleday. She currently works as a producer for HBO's *America Undercover* series.